Ben McConnell / Jackie Huba

Authors of *Creating Customer Evangelists*

CITIZEN
MARKETERS

When People Are
the Message

KAPLAN PUBLISHING

This publication is designed to provide accurate and authoritative information in regard to the subject matter covered. It is sold with the understanding that the publisher is not engaged in rendering legal, accounting, or other professional service. If legal advice or other expert assistance is required, the services of a competent professional should be sought.

Editorial Director: Jennifer Farthing
Acquisitions Editor: Karen Murphy
Production Editor: Samantha Raue
Typesetter: Todd Bowman
Cover Designer: Gail Chandler

Published by Kaplan Publishing,
a division of Kaplan, Inc.

Printed in the United States of America

07 08 09 10 9 8 7 6 5 4 3 2

Library of Congress Cataloging-in-Publication Data

McConnell, Ben.
  Citizen marketers : when people are the message / Ben McConnell and Jackie Huba.
    p. cm.
  Includes bibliographical references and index.
  ISBN-13: 978-1-4195-9606-3
  ISBN-10: 1-4195-9606-3
  1. Customer relations. 2. Social media. 3. Social media--Economic aspects. 4. Internet--Social aspects. 5. Interactive marketing. I. Huba, Jackie. II. Title.
  HF5415.5.M1833 2006
  658.8'12--dc22   2006030817

Kaplan Publishing books are available at special quantity discounts to use for sales promotions, employee premiums, or educational purposes. Please call our Special Sales Department to order or for more information at 800-621-9621, ext. 4444, e-mail *kaplanpubsales@kaplan.com,* or write to Kaplan Publishing, 30 South Wacker Drive, Suite 2500, Chicago, IL 60606-7481.

CONTENTS

To see the work of the citizen marketers featured
in this book, go to *citizenmarketers.com*.

In November 2004, a California man by the name of George Masters uploaded a file to his personal Web site that would change his life and the worldview of many people about the convergence of technology, marketing, and pop culture. The file was "Tiny Machine," a 60-second animation Masters had spent five months creating that features as its star an acrobatic iPod, the portable music player from Apple Computer.

Describing "Tiny Machine" is like describing an abstract painting, but its animation is not unlike 1960s-era candy-colored kaleidoscopes whose lenses diffuse animated hearts that morph into iPods. The portable music players zig and zag in hairpin turns and spin like dizzying calliopes. All of it is choreographed to a pop-trippy song from the 1980s. As an ad, "Tiny Machine" is all branding. No narration or explanations of features. It's wonderfully designed and professionally executed eye candy. A portfolio piece.

Given Apple's history of a rainbow-inspired logo, the "Tiny Machine" ad could have fit in with some of the company's advertising efforts. So, a casual observer might not have been faulted for seeing "Tiny Machine" as the work of a hot creative director inventing a new, albeit retro, iPod branding schema for Apple, hoping it would wash across the American pop culture landscape like many of the company's previous efforts had. But "Tiny Machine" would never show up as a television ad, its imagery reinforced by magazine ads or giant posters in the windows of Apple's stores. George Masters was an Orange County, California, vocational-school teacher and an amateur digital animator who was playing with software to improve his craft. He posted "Tiny Machine" to the Web and asked a handful of Mac fan sites for feedback on his work; he'd been a long-time Apple customer and enthusiast, so the iPod was a natural model for his study. Word of his ad spread quickly among fan sites dedicated to Apple Macintosh products.

Then "Tiny Machine" showed up on MetaFilter, a community Web site whose tens of thousands of members share links and discuss interesting sites. That's where Gary Stein saw it. He was working as an online advertising analyst for Jupiter Research at the time and wrote about it on his blog. "You could take this thing and put it on MTV this afternoon. It's not only good, it's good advertising. People go to college to learn this. He just gets it," said Stein at the time. A handful of marketing bloggers picked up on Stein's recommendation and within a few weeks the "ad" was cruising through the Internet's word-of-mouth jet stream. As word spread from blog to blog, "Tiny Machine" sparked the interest of newspaper and magazine writers and television producers, who featured Masters in stories and interview segments. Instead of Apple infecting the landscape of pop culture, Masters's "Tiny Machine" ad infected the imaginations of marketers whose work often tries to influence culture.

Within a month, "Tiny Machine" had been viewed online more than 500,000 times. It eventually led to a job offer for Masters—from a California production company—to create animations full time. He accepted.

The story of Masters and his "Tiny Machine" ad represents the potential for everyday people to create work that gets sucked into the swirling new universe of blogs, podcasts, and specialized online communities, allowing them to build new and unprecedented levels of recognition, even fame. "Tiny Machine" arrived at a point when millions of people in home offices, cubicles, schools, and coffee shops around the world were writing essays, taking photos, creating animations, shooting videos, and covering news as amateurs. They were using an emerging Web-based publishing platform called social media that enabled people to talk, discuss, share, and find new communities of like-minded people. November 2004 marked the dawning of a new form of amateur culture that is bypassing many of the traditional media gatekeepers of radio, television, and print who determine hits, stars, and what the masses consume. Now, everyday people are having real and tangible effects on culture that has largely been controlled by traditional media. New voices are discovered, stars are born, and the existing media barons of culture are wondering how everything changed so quickly.

Citizen Marketers is the story of how amateurs and professionals commingle to assume new forms of ownership in the companies, brands, products, and people they closely follow, disrupting the traditions of the existing cultural filters and promoters. It's also the story of how some organizations have embraced the new reality of participatory engagement, tossing aside the old model of the passive consumer. That George Masters could ride a wave of iPod mania and fulfill a dream of a new career thanks to the technological convenience of people-powered media illustrates a shift when media became social. Widespread publishing and distribution of a cool idea, a new product, or a hot new animation was no longer the domain of big, traditional media. It was around this time, in November 2004, that the very idea of media itself was evolving into a two-way, three-way, and multiple-way ecosystem of gossip, ideas, news, and collaboration. Everyday people could be publishers *and* broadcasters *and* audience members.

Until this time, most traditional media had been the postal carriers of news and entertainment, using a delivery system marked by limited options of interaction. But blogs, podcasts, and photo and video sharing sites convert news and entertainment into a playground of connection, where readers can comment and interact easily and immediately with publishers. Or link to specific stories, videos, or communities and point thousands of others toward it. It is the creation of content on top of content, where ease is paramount and many democratic principles are sacrosanct, that is fueling the rise of social media. Social media remove a great number of traditional barriers to widespread distribution. Millions of people use the new, *new* media toolset to discuss, debate, and collaborate with one another as millions more watch, listen, and learn.

When media became social, it was natural to call it social media, which we have come to define as the sum total of people who create content online, as well as the people who interact with it or one another. People use social media to express their opinions, their creativity, or news about their hobbies and altogether "socialize" with friends, peers, and strangers. They are building their own audiences, the size of which is rivaling those of traditional media. As social media spread and subvert the traditional media, they pose fundamental new challenges for companies and brands accustomed to closely stage-managing their reputations.

When his new Inspiron 600M laptop arrived in the mail from Dell Computer, Jeff Jarvis found that it didn't work very well. Once powered up, it was hot to the touch and unbearably slow. Jarvis called Dell and asked the company to send a technician to his home in New York and repair it. After all, he'd paid a premium for a four-year, in-home service warranty for just this type of problem. The technician who arrived to fix the computer found it was so broken he couldn't fix it. The only solution, the technician said, was to send the machine back to the factory. That lit Jarvis's fuse. He'd been a professional critic for years, working at various points in his career as a critic for *TV Guide* and then *People* magazine. He later founded the magazine *Entertainment Weekly*. He was the type of person and writer who was not bashful about sharing his opinion.

Before blogs and the Internet, Jarvis would have had three recourses to resolving the problem of a new-but-broken laptop and poor technical support: Write a letter of complaint to the company, call the company's customer hotline, or alert the Better Business Bureau. But Jarvis was a well-known blogger. He typed a furious and angry note to the world:

> Dell lies. Dell sucks. I just got a new Dell laptop and paid a fortune for the four-year, in-home service. The machine is a lemon and the service is a lie. I'm having all kinds of trouble with the hardware. . . . But what really irks me is that they say if they sent someone to my home—which I paid for—he wouldn't have the parts, so I might as well just send the machine and lose it for seven to ten days—plus the time going through this crap. . . . DELL SUCKS. DELL LIES. Put that in your Google and smoke it, Dell.

He posted it to his blog at *Buzzmachine.com* on June 21, 2005. Hundreds of his blog readers commented on the post, many angrily sharing their own similar experiences with Dell. He wrote another post two days later, explaining how Dell had asked him to remove the hard drive before he sent the machine back to the factory. That didn't make sense to him, so like a pack of firecrackers, Jarvis went off again. He titled his second post, "Dell Hell, continued." After two days of repairs, Dell returned the laptop. The overheating wasn't fixed (154 degrees, according to a thermometer program he found), and it was still dreadfully slow. "And I'm getting e-mail from Dell people who clearly are not paying attention," he wrote in yet another post. "'Dear Mr. Langley,' said one. I corrected them and said the name's Jarvis. The response: 'Dear Ms. Kolar.'"

With near-daily updates about his ongoing laptop troubles, "Dell Hell" became a virus that infected parts of culture. Within a week, "Dell Hell" was a topic of panel discussions at several technology and marketing conferences. "Dell Hell" was the subject of stories in the *Washington Post,* the *Guardian,* the *Wall Street Journal,* and the *New York Times.* "Dell Hell" had become a catalyst for other people to share their own bad experiences with Dell on their blogs. "Dell Hell" even convinced me (Jackie) to steer clear of Dell for a computer purchase of my own. But "Dell Hell" was actually a symptom of bigger problems at Dell.

Competitors selling PCs had largely matched Dell's prices and raised their own service levels by the end of 2004, leaving little room for Windows-based computer companies to differentiate themselves. Dell lost its low-price advantage, part of which involved taking financial shortcuts with customer service. That caught up with them. A year after Jarvis's first blog entries, Google counted more than 10 million references to "Dell Hell," and the company's stock price had dropped 45 percent. Jeff Jarvis's one-man marketing campaign spurred thousands of people to chime in with similar stories on blogs, news Web sites, and online communities. "We are in the new era of 'seller beware,'" Jarvis wrote on his blog. "Now when you screw your customers, your customers can fight back and publish and organize."

Almost a year after Jarvis's first post, Dell announced it would invest $100 million to improve its customer service. Shortly after that, Dell launched its own blog "to learn and improve by listening to customers." Bloggers who had posted their own stories about problems with their Dell computers started receiving phone calls from company "resolution experts," hoping to stem some of the anti-Dell venom that was coursing through their veins. Dell couldn't afford to ignore the discussions any longer.

Would Dell ever fix Jarvis's new laptop? He didn't wait to find out. He bought a Mac.

The stories of Masters and Jarvis illustrate a fundamental characteristic about social media: it exponentially multiplies the power of one. A lone person today has a significantly better chance of influencing other people not only in her immediate network of friends and peers, but in the school, work, and social networks of the world than she did before the arrival of social media. A lone person today has a greater chance to create widespread excitement or disrupt a company's reputation without the assistance of the big megaphones of traditional media. A lone person today can create significant and measurable ripples in the reputations of companies, reputations increasingly monitored by stockholders, industry analysts, *and* the traditional media. And thanks to Google, a lone person can create a multi-layered, anthropological impression of a moment in time for thousands, if not millions of other people to read and absorb immediately, months or years from now. The funnel of the message megaphone is a lot wider.

Social media turned George Masters into a hot item for several weeks. Social media allowed Jeff Jarvis to catalyze thousands of people to spread an idea, encapsulated in a slogan, so far and wide that it culminated in Dell spending $100 million to re-engineer its customer service operation.

The stories of Masters, Jarvis, and others we'll tell also illustrate several fundamental shifts taking place in technology, sociology, and the pop culture of media creation, attention, and interaction. Social media is calling into question the very definition of media itself, for it is media that affects our culture, and culture affects what we buy. The debate is being accelerated by the fast-moving winds of technology growth and free speech. In *Citizen Marketers,* we'll introduce you to everyday people—who are everywhere and in far greater numbers than you think—who create content on behalf of products, brands, companies, or people. Sometimes they create authoritative and professional content in concert with the companies in question, but most often it's by themselves or with a community of colleagues or friends. Collectively, the work of citizen marketers has the potential to affect the culture of business. In *Citizen Marketers,* we'll explain the motivations of content creators and their aggravations in the face of indifferent or distant companies. We'll share data about the number of people who are creating content online and describe in plain, nontechnical language the tools they use. And finally, we'll explore the collaborative and participatory models of several organizations that are embracing citizen marketers. We'll learn how their open governance fuels their growth, including one company whose entire manufacturing model is driven by the votes of its customer-citizens. To understand how and why we have arrived at this moment in social media history, we must understand who the citizen marketers are and the types and capabilities of their work.

CHAPTER ONE

Filters, Fanatics, Facilitators, and Firecrackers

It is the business of the future to be dangerous. . . . The major advances in civilization are processes that all but wreck the societies in which they occur.

A. N. Whitehead, *The Self-Organizing Universe*

Fiona Apple was frantic. Someone secretly slipped her newly recorded album to a radio DJ, and he was playing it on the air. The problem was the album hadn't been released yet. In fact, Apple wasn't sure if the album was ever going to be released. That a DJ was now playing it for a substantial audience in Seattle put the future of her album, and possibly her career, in jeopardy.

She had recorded a collection of new songs in 2003 and called it *Extraordinary Machine*. It was the follow-up work to her two previous albums of confessional, introspective songs that had won her praise from critics and plenty of adoring fans. Both albums were commercially successful, but it had been four years before she had started recording *Extraordinary Machine*, a lifetime in pop music. After some prodding by a producer-collaborator to start writing and composing again, Apple returned to the studio with aplomb. She recorded new songs and then . . . hated them. Didn't like their sound. A bigger problem: Neither did Sony, her record label.

So Apple's collaborator introduced her to a new producer. He tinkered with a few of the songs and gave them a new sound. She liked what she heard. Right there she decided the best plan was to rerecord the album with the new producer. It's an artist's prerogative to change her mind, but Sony balked. It didn't want to pay for rerecording an album it had already paid once to record and didn't like. Discussions went back and forth. According to Apple, the label offered to pay for rerecording the first song it liked, then pay individually for other songs it liked. No deal, she said. As an artist, she considered herself a better expert on musical aesthetics than the businessmen of Sony. So she asked another label to buy out her contract. Those talks broke down. Her spirit broken, Apple gave up. She figured her career was over and considering quitting, going so far as to apply for an internship with an organization called Green Chimneys, which uses farm animals as therapy for troubled kids.

It wasn't too much later that the Seattle DJ was trumpeting his coup. The DJ may have fueled word of mouth about the new album, but Apple feared it would destroy her chances with another label buying her contract. Who would buy songs that had already been heard with their digital files perhaps already spreading on the Internet? Things weren't looking good for Fiona Apple.

The impasse fueled a number of conspiracy theories, especially the theory that Sony didn't like the album and wanted to cut its losses by not releasing it, which was partly true. Then *FreeFiona.com* popped up.

Described as "an international organization campaigning to Sony for the release of Fiona Apple's new album," the Web site was the work of a 21-year-old Columbia, Missouri, musician and music teacher named Dave Muscato. Describing himself as a Fiona

Apple fan since the age of 12 and claiming "no special relationship with her," Muscato rallied fellow fans to pressure Sony into releasing *Extraordinary Machine*. He assembled ten assistants from an existing fan forum for the artist, and his claim of an "international" organization wasn't just hype. His assistants were from Israel, Mexico, Italy, South America, and Scotland as well as four American states. They launched their grassroots organization in November 2004. Within a few months, they'd convinced 36,000 people to sign a petition. They sent Sony a refrigerator-sized box filled with plastic apples, each one inscribed with the name of a petition signer. They organized a demonstration outside Sony's offices in New York on a cold January day in 2005, chanting with 45 other clenched-fist fans, "We want Fiona!"

Apple's recollection of the event: "I remember very clearly going into the back room of my mother's apartment and my sister was sitting at the computer. I said, 'Look up Free Fiona.' First I started laughing, saying, 'This is hilarious; people are protesting and I'm sitting on my ass watching reruns of *Columbo*. I'm not on the phone with my lawyers trying to get my album released. I'm applying at Green Chimneys! And then I started crying because I really felt touched. It's an incredible feeling to feel like all these people who you don't know care about you. And it was bigger than me. It was about what was going on in the music industry and anybody deciding what's sellable."

Muscato spent $1,000 to build the Web site, purchase the plastic apples, and organize the rally. He opened a PayPal account to solicit donations. Like a nonprofit organization, he was transparent about his mission, goals, and expenses: "Plastic apples: $1,033.62 so far." He raised $3,280.56. Not quite the $8,825 he'd hoped, which would pay for all of the expenses, but better than nothing, even if the campaign ended up costing him about $3,000 of his own money. The plan worked; *FreeFiona.com* caught the attention of *Rolling Stone* and the *New York Times*, which wrote about the New York City rally.

That was the clincher. Not long after, Sony agreed to pay to rerecord the album. Apple completed the work in a few weeks, and Sony released *Extraordinary Machine* on October 5, 2005. It debuted at number seven on the *Billboard* charts and was later nominated for a Grammy Award. "Apple credits all the press attention from the Free Fiona campaign for spooking her label into finally giving her the money and creative freedom to rerecord the album on her terms," *Entertainment Weekly* later reported. In January 2006 *Extraordinary Machine* was certified gold, meaning it had sold at least 500,000 copies.

~

Citizen marketers create what could be considered marketing and advertising content on behalf of people, brands, products, or organizations. Often they invite others to participate in their marketing work. Dave Muscato created a Web site and an actionable cause on behalf of Fiona Apple. His small but influential group delivered results for someone—Fiona Apple—about whom they felt passionate. Considering that Muscato spent thousands of dollars of his own to help someone he had never met, Muscato may not be considered a typical fan. That's the nature of citizen marketers—they don't often represent the average person, member, customer, or citizen. They are on the fringes, driven by passion, creativity, and a sense of duty. Like a concerned citizen.

Everyone feels passionate about someone or something; judging the appropriateness of someone's passion is a subjective debate, and making such value judgments is not our intent. Instead, we aim to introduce you to people like Dave Muscato who create content and collaborate with others on behalf of people, brands, products, or organizations. The Dave Muscatos of the world are undertaking citizen marketer work with increasing frequency and influence. Muscato's reason why? "I'm an indie musician and I know firsthand that just a few dedicated people with passion, inspiration, and a common goal can change the world, to paraphrase Eleanor Roosevelt." Anyone whose livelihood is affected by the swells of popular culture should take notice and be prepared.

Among the world of citizen marketers, Muscato is a Fanatic. He is a true believer, an evangelist. His work falls comfortably into the middle of what we call the four *F*s: Filters, Fanatics, Facilitators, and Firecrackers. The first three *F*s are the noble worker bees of citizen marketers, focusing for months or years at a time on their work. The Firecrackers, well, they are what they sound like—citizen marketers who explode loudly and mightily and then vanish in a puff of smoke. We begin with the Filters.

1.

The Filters are human wire services. They collect traditional media stories, bloggers' rants and raves, podcasts, or fan creations about a specific company or brand and then package this information into a daily or near-daily stream of links, story summaries, and observations. Most Filters maintain a steady objectivity like traditional news wire services, but some Filters cross over into analysis. For the most part, Filters are not prone to fits of pique or confrontation, and they occasionally produce their own journalistic work. Like the HackingNetflix blog, for example.

Mike Kaltschnee has been writing HackingNetflix since November 2004. Each day, he composes three to five posts that could be considered plot points on the company's DVD-by-mail subscription business. Some 7,000 readers follow along daily. He and a slew of collaborative readers (he estimates about half of his news items are submitted by readers) highlight the company's marketing tactics, such as "Netflix sponsors Google Videos" and "Netflix monster house banners." He often describes challenges to Netflix's business model: "Blockbuster $2.99 store rentals" and "TiVo testing movie downloads." He posts stories about the company's challenges to delivering consistent customer service: "Netflix rental history controversy" and "Netflix customer support on throttling." Finally, he highlights a lot of new movies available on DVD through Netflix.

In the world of investment banking, well-paid analysts undertake somewhat similar work, trying to connect the dots of a business on behalf of investors who hold millions of shares. Why would someone do the same thing for free? Kaltschnee, who works for a stock-photo agency during the day, describes his motivation for launching the site: "An experiment in company and community relations. I'm a fan of Netflix and wanted to learn more about the company, sharing what I found," he notes. "It may have started as a fan site, but I've tried to make it more professional and even—shudder—'fair and balanced.'" His work is not unlike an analyst teaching himself and others the business he monitors. That's the basis of the hacking metaphor: it borrows a computer programmer's term to take something apart in order to understand how it works, not how to infiltrate and exploit. (The exploiters are usually called "crackers" or "black hats." On every HackingNetflix page, a disclaimer says the site "will not teach you how to lie, cheat, or steal from Netflix.")

In that sense, HackingNetflix is like an independent news operation whose nightly top story is how Netflix is doing. He and other Filters adamantly stay on topic (HackingNetflix does occasionally cover news about Blockbuster Online), and they reflect a journalist's focus on timeliness and speed. Kaltschnee writes short posts with the objective air of a professional journalist. While he has conducted interviews with Netflix employees, including CEO and founder Reed Hastings, and often posts items about company job openings, Kaltschnee's singular focus has heightened his authority as a Netflix monitor. Traditional media journalists often quote him to provide contextual understanding when writing about the company or the industry. Search for Netflix on Google and HackingNetflix is the usually up high on the first page of results. Kaltschnee's role of blogger-as-publisher is similar to what traditional newspapers do: he does not own stock in Netflix or Blockbuster and pays "full retail price for my subscriptions." As a publisher, he also earns income from ads on the blog and revenue from the affiliate program Netflix (and Blockbuster) pays to those who create links on their own sites that lead to Netflix memberships.

As a category, the Filters present an interesting future; their work could be called amateur brand journalism, and sometimes amateurs turn pro. Dennis Lloyd, a civil draftsman and graphic designer, started *iPodLounge.com* as an independent Filter a few days after Apple introduced the iPod in 2001. Now called *iLounge.com,* the site has become quite popular; about 4 million people visit each month, and 100,000 of them participate in its forums. Advertising revenue enabled Lloyd to quit his day job and work full time on the site. He has two full-time employees.

Jim Romenesko runs StarbucksGossip. It's his hobby blog since he blogs as an employee of the nonprofit Poynter Institute, a journalism education and research institute. Poynter had lured him away from the world of newspapers to blog about journalism news and issues. Romenesko says he was inspired to start StarbucksGossip "after overhearing some interesting employee-customer discussions, and figuring they'd translate well on a Web site," he told us via e-mail, presumably from a Starbucks.

"I started the site to prompt conversations between Starbucks employees, customers (fans), and critics. I think I've succeeded, although my sense is the employees and fans outnumber the critics 10-1." He's also a Starbucks regular, shuttling between three to five different stores every day. "I see it as a good place for me to do my work and get a decent cup of drip coffee. Also, I thought someone should track Starbucks news, simply because it's such a force in business and popular culture." With a tagline that says, "Monitoring America's favorite drug dealer," StarbucksGossip focuses on stories that introduce new drink menus, problems at stores or locales, marketing programs, unionizing efforts, quarterly results, or the odd but interesting feature. His posts may generate a handful of comments or dozens; a post about tipping generated more than 1,000 comments. Many comments seem to come from Starbucks employees.

When Starbucks reported lower quarterly sales growth in August 2006, it blamed wait times caused by an expanded menu of blended beverages. On StarbucksGossip, people who sounded a lot like Starbucks employees expressed their frustration. "The problem is that blender drinks take longer to make than espresso drinks, and unlike espresso drinks, there's very little you can do to speed the process up," wrote one person. "Plus every time you turn around there's yet another new blended drink coming out and another promotion campaign to try to push more of them out the door. Can't we just go back to being a coffee company?" Said another person, "The funny thing is, store partners have been telling upper management for years that blended slows speed of service but no one upstairs seemed to want to hear it. Maybe they'll listen now."

This points toward an interesting dynamic about Starbucks-Gossip: it seems to have evolved into an employee-discussion forum. One visitor shared his store-management strategy, using lingo obvious to employees: "It drives me nuts when I see a barista standing at the espresso bar with no drinks while his or her counterpart is slaving away on Cold Beverage Station. The espresso barista should help the Cold Bevs until more espresso drinks are called. Or the floater should do just what the title says and float, not just call drinks over." A former Starbucks retail-marketing manager who went on to write a book about his company experiences calls StarbucksGossip the best source for employee feedback. "Despite all the processes Starbucks has put in place for employees to provide feedback to corporate decision-makers, the truest feedback channel is outside of Starbucks channels," wrote John Moore, on his own blog called Brand Autopsy. "Starbucks' truest feedback channel is on the StarbucksGossip blog." Future employees doing a bit of research on the company as a potential employer are bound to stumble on StarbucksGossip; it's usually up high on the first page of Google search results for Starbucks. (Ironically, it's often followed by a site called *ihatestarbucks.com*, another amateur-operated site that has posted thousands of anti-Starbucks essays written by its visitors.)

Like the other Filters we have identified, Romenesko wants the several thousand people who visit StarbucksGossip each day to share and debate their opinions. "I usually don't inject my opinion, except on rare occasions. Once was when I started hearing Christmas music in the Starbucks stores in early November. The next year the music didn't start until Thanksgiving. I don't know if my complaints had anything to do with that, but I was pleased whatever the case."

Andrew Carton, a British entrepreneur and consultant, launched *Treonauts.com* in November 2004 as a "bloguide." It is dedicated to the Treo, a combination personal digital assistant and cell phone made by Palm. Carton is a prodigious Filter: he reviews each new version of the product, showcases tips and tricks on using the product, highlights the latest news from cellular providers who sell the PDA, and discusses product accessories and software. The site says it hosts 300,000 visitors per month. One of its fans is Harry McCracken, the editor of *PC World* magazine. "It's an unusually entertaining and informative blog, by a user who's passionate about this product, its uses, and its future—and who isn't afraid to talk about its downsides. I'm not sure if there's such a thing as Treo spirit, but if there is, Treonauts definitely has it."

Asif Alibhai has set out to catalog and serve every piece of Apple Computer video advertising ever created. His *WatchMacTV.com* Web site stores hundreds of videos about Apple. Every "Hello, I'm a PC," ad, every iPod and iTunes ad, every "Switch commercial," and every pop-culture video reference he can find. He's a Filter who's also a collector, and his hobby fills his free time when he's not busy as a student in London. He sends the tens of thousands of subscribers to his podcast and videocast the latest Apple-themed video he has acquired. "Aside from all of the commercials Apple has released, there are hundreds of rare and unreleased videos that people don't know about," he says. If you have one, Alibhai would like a copy.

But why Apple? "That's a very hard question to answer," he says. "It's like the moment you get a Mac, you're in love with the company and everything they do."

2.

The Fanatics are true believers and evangelists. Their roles as citizen marketers may include filtering work, but they love to analyze the daily or weekly progress of a brand, product, organization, or person and prescribe courses of action. They are, essentially, volunteer coaches. The Fanatics praise great company efforts—which may vary widely from marketing to accessory development—but they will also criticize mistakes and lapses in full view of the world, just like a coach may do as a teaching tool. The personalities of the Fanatics are as varied as the personalities in sports coaching, too. Just as college basketball coach Bobby Knight has a personality (tends to be explosive) that's vastly different than pro football coach Tony Dungy (tends to be even-keeled), both ultimately want their teams to excel and win.

Take *McChronicles.com,* for instance, a blog written by a New York man who focuses exclusively on McDonald's. He wants McDonald's to be "awesome." With a good deal of care, he critiques the company's marketing and branding work and conducts regular secret-shopper reviews of McDonald's stores in his regular-job travels. He grades stores on service, food preparation, and cleanliness. Woe to the McDonald's operator whose poorly maintained bathroom he discovers; McChronicles seldom forgives that transgression. His review of a McDonald's in San Francisco's historic Haight-Ashbury hippie district is direct: "Regions with far less (of note) to brag about do a much better job of reflecting their tradition or community than this store does. What should be a landmark is actually a disappointment."

He is anonymous, though. Although that's uncommon among most citizen marketers (we will introduce you to a woman who anonymously blogs about Target), his reasons for anonymity are based on the stakes of his livelihood. He told us in an e-mail that he lives and works in a relatively small city; therefore, "many of my McDonald's experiences are in and around my town. One man owns about 30 McDonald's here. The owner of my company is that man's friend. Both are very rich and powerful." He started the blog in January 2005 because of what he calls "a love-hate relationship" with the brand.

"McDonald's is one of the most significant brands in my life," he told us. "It plays a big role in my past—especially in my childhood (it's almost like Christmas). Secondly, it is a shame to see the once-splendid brand miss the mark of what I always felt it was, what they told me it was, and what it could be. So much of what they do is right—they're so close to being awesome for so many people around the globe—that it hurts to see them just miss the mark. I just want them to 'get it,' and achieve it so that so many people can be really happy (including the employees). Actually, I am sure that many employees get it but feel their hands are tied by corporate, legal, the system—just like in other companies.

"I guess you could say I just want McDonald's to be awesome."

The work of the McChronicles blogger follows an interesting trend among the Fanatics. A somewhat disproportionate number of the citizen marketer sites we cataloged focus on brands in the food and beverage industries. Michael Marx runs a fan blog dedicated to Barq's root beer at *Barqsman.com.* He is a married, 35-year-old Gilbert, Arizona, resident with three daughters who says he has been drinking Barq's since his college days. (By day, he is the research manager for a trade magazine.) Like many of our other examples, he started blogging in November 2004, too. His purpose was to learn how to blog. But why focus on Barq's? "To keep the brand alive."

He seeks out and publishes a variety of oddities about Barq's, like a recipe for cooking ribs in the soda or lamps and birdhouses for sale on eBay made from empty cans of Barq's. He is a thoughtful reviewer of Barq's advertising and Web marketing. His review of Barq's redesigned Web site praises an animated Barqy the Dog mascot and its video games. He criticizes a lack of product and nutritional information and wonders why history about the 116-year-old brand is scarce. Search for Barq's on the all-important Google, and his site is usually listed third, after the offical Barq's site and a Wikipedia entry for the beverage. Marx may love Barq's, but Barq's doesn't return the affection. The Coca-Cola Company, which owns Barq's, makes several appearances in *Citizen Marketers*. It tends to make products that everyday people enjoy talking about, analyzing, or playing with. Coca-Cola does not engage in conversation with its fans or citizen marketers. The company has never contacted Marx, and as we'll see with two other examples, it tends to ignore or dismiss the work of everyday people.

Marx is undeterred. When an e-mail arrived from the Green Bay Packers, he took notice. A star player on the NFL team was "in need" of his favorite home-state root beer, and the team asked Marx to help the player locate a case of it. Marx called Barq's biggest collector in Mississippi, who rounded up three cases of bottled Barq's and shipped it to Green Bay. "It was a good feeling to be able to help a fellow Barq's drinker get his fix so far away from home," Marx told us.

Food is a popular subject for the Fanatics, but entertainment is probably more popular. The Disney Blog is the focus for a Fanatic who covers the company's latest corporate news, how hurricanes affect theme park business, and recent Disney DVD releases. John Frost writes the Disney Blog. By day, he works for a charity in Orlando, Florida, that provides cost-free Walt Disney World vacations to children with life-threatening illnesses. That creates an interesting intersection between his hobby (the Disney Blog) and his work (taking sick kids to Disney World). He is married, with kids, and describes himself as a "third-generation Disney fan." He started the blog in June 2004 because he "saw a total lack of any Disney fandom represented in the blogosphere." In his "Fan Video of the Week" series, he catalogs videos made by other Disney fanatics. One video was a 23-minute history of the Magic Kingdom's Tomorrowland park, documenting its opening in 1971 and its life through the mid-1990s. Another is a 16-minute video diary of a French couple exploring Disneyland Paris. Don't miss the video made by two interns in Walt Disney World's College

Program documenting their internship, which seems to include a fair amount of drinking.

It's not uncommon for Fanatics to assume an activist role, as Dave Muscato did on behalf of Fiona Apple. For as long as TV shows have been around, Fanatics for them have a well-documented history of surfacing when a series is cancelled.

Fans of the WB Television Network's fantasy thriller *Angel* raised more than $41,000 in 2004 to convince the network to return the show for a sixth season. Fans used the money to rent mobile billboards in Los Angeles that read, "We'll follow *Angel* to hell . . . or another network." They took out ads in the show-business trade magazines *Variety* and the *Hollywood Reporter,* and they sent 2,000 chocolate bars with the *SavingAngel.org* logo and slogan to Warner Bros., Fox, TNT, and other network executives. But all of the networks passed, and *Angel* went to TV show heaven.

Fans of the TV comedy *Arrested Development* sent thousands of banana-shaped stress balls (the family in the show once owned a frozen banana stand) to Fox executives, hoping they would reconsider their decision to cancel the show. Fox stood firm and the show stayed dead. Fans of *Star Trek: Enterprise* were monetarily serious about their fandom: they raised more than $3 million in 2005 to help Paramount continue production of a fifth season. Paramount declined the money, and the show died.

When loyal fans of HBO's gritty western *Deadwood*—a show called "one of the highest quality shows in the history of television"— heard in May 2006 that it would end unexpectedly after three seasons, they mobilized. But *Deadwood's* fanatical citizen marketers and the maturation of social media may have helped craft a rare ending to the typical outcome of a Hollywood cancellation story.

Neil Monnens, a Fanatic living in San Francisco, launched a site called *HboNoMo.com*. It was an online petition for its signatories to pledge the cancellation of their HBO subscriptions if the network did not renew *Deadwood*. It gathered 652 signatures in 13 days. Hundreds of passionate and thoughtful opinions were written: "I've been a subscriber since 1982. There have been many good shows on HBO, but none better than *Deadwood*," wrote one signer of the petition. "The decision to cancel *Deadwood* shows HBO's complete disrespect for its audience and for the artists who produced this great show. I will not support a business that treats its consumers with such disdain."

Chip Collins, in Boston, launched a Web site called *SaveDeadwood.net*. In five days, he raised $6,000 from 81 fans to publish a letter in *Variety*. It read: "In our opinion, failing to allow *Deadwood* to complete its full intended story not only deprives millions of HBO subscribers around the world of the opportunity to see *Deadwood* to its rightful conclusion, it also creates a serious disincentive to viewer investment in future HBO series." They signed their letter, "*Current* HBO Subscribers." Considering the show's rich regard for profanity, it's not difficult to imagine the expletive-filled e-mails that streamed into HBO's offices.

As is often the case in the complex and multilayered business of making entertainment, the reasons behind *Deadwood*'s demise were not so much about the show's popularity—its 4 million viewers made it HBO's second-most-watched show after *The Sopranos,* with 9 million viewers—but about the economics of the future. HBO didn't own all of the show's distribution rights, where networks earn substantial profits. In what sounds like a complicated trade of baseball players, *Deadwood* creator David Milch had been under contract with Paramount when HBO wanted to buy his script for the show. When making their deal, HBO gave Paramount foreign distribution rights to *Deadwood* to acquire Milch. Even though Paramount had no investment in the show, it has reaped some benefits of its subsequent success. Splitting profits with Paramount meant HBO wasn't making as much money on the show as it might have.

Meanwhile, Milch developed an idea for an altogether new series. HBO loved it and signed it immediately, including all distribution rights. But here's the part that perplexed TV critics: HBO wanted Milch to begin work immediately on the new series rather than complete a fourth season of *Deadwood*. Working on both shows simultaneously would be virtually impossible for the hands-on Milch, and HBO didn't want to pay contracted *Deadwood* actors to wait until the new show had finished shooting. When HBO confirmed on May 11, 2006, that it had let the options on contracts with *Deadwood's* large cast lapse, fans knew the third season, which was just about to start, would be its last. That's when some of them joined the ranks of TV-show activists.

Catalyzing people toward action has grown to be significantly easier in the age of social media because there are more opportunities for conversation to build and spread. Some 30 fan forums on various Web sites, including *HBO.com,* were already dedicated to discussing all things *Deadwood*. Even forums dedicated to entirely different subjects, like Full Contact Poker, talked about the show. With fans throughout multiple online communities, news of the "save *Deadwood*" campaign spread quickly. Online forums typically archive all discussions so fans can jump into a discussion at any point, suggest a course of action, and test its viability with the community. This open architecture creates a transparent form of collected knowledge. The delivery mechanisms built into many social media tools accelerate knowledge sharing. When collective knowledge is created at a faster rate, decisions can be made comparably faster, potentially resulting in faster action. And that may be how *Deadwood's* fans made a difference.

Almost a month later, HBO and Milch agreed to two, two-hour final episodes to be aired sometime in 2007 that would conclude the series. At least one person involved in the show gives the Fanatics credit for forcing HBO's hand. W. Earl Brown, who plays

Deadwood's tough-guy Dan Dority, often chats with fans on the HBO online forums. After news of the compromise was announced, he wrote: "Well, y'all did it. I honestly believe that y'all's efforts were the final straw that pushed things toward finishing *Deadwood*—not ending it."

Chip Collins, who had raised the money for the ad in *Variety*, later said of his activism work, "It's hard to think of many fan campaigns to save shows that have worked. But we really went into this with the idea that we want to make a statement. We want to go down fighting." Like many of the characters on *Deadwood*, they did.

The stories of the Fanatics illustrate a central theme: they want to contribute. They face vastly different challenges in their quest to add value, whether it's time or indifference. But they want to contribute and often do so, even if the company isn't listening.

3.

Facilitators are community creators. Their primary citizen marketer tool is a Web-based bulletin board or community software. Facilitators are like the mayors of online towns, and some online communities exceed the populations of small cities.

Facilitators create online communities for several reasons. For products such as the Palm Treo smartphone or the TiVo digital video recorder, those product communities are de facto support groups where customers act as call-center technicians. Some Facilitators create communities simply for fans to connect with other fans. Some communities do both. The size or demographics of some Facilitator-created communities becomes attractive enough to interest advertisers.

Most Facilitators are independent of the company or product, but a few have sought the company's blessing or tacit approval. At least one company—TiVo—maintains regular online and offline conversations with members of a citizen marketer community dedicated to the product. Its founder is David Bott. He was a 33-year-old home-theater enthusiast and municipal employee in a small town near Rochester, New York, when he launched TiVo-Community in January 1999 for fans of the digital video recording device. Several TiVo employees are visible regulars among Bott's community of 130,000 members.

Communities for specific models of cars are a particular favorite of the Facilitators. Online you'll find citizen-created sites for Chevrolet's Corvette, Ford's Thunderbird and Explorer (one Ford Explorer club is organized solely to conduct charitable work), and Nissan's Maxima and Z28, and the list goes on. If there's a model of car, there's probably a citizen-created forum for it.

A Facilitator-created forum for BMW's Mini Cooper is called *MINI2.com*. It bills itself as the largest online community for Mini owners. Paul Mullett was a 24-year-old full-time dad in Bedfordshire, England, and Casey Swenson was a 25-year-old programmer at IBM in Rochester, Minnesota, when they launched *MINI2.com* in January 2001 as an independent venture. Over the years, their community grew to 20,000 Mini enthusiasts from around the world who share in the ups and downs of owning the petite car. The *MINI2.com* community is more elaborate than comparable communities; members can pay $17 (that's 10 British pounds or 15 Euros) to become a MINI2 Privilege Member. The fee allows members to upload images, access a private forum for other paying members, create a personal blog, and get discounts from Mini aftermarket companies. For Mullett and Swenson, being Facilitators means catering to paying members and policing the community in search of those who would disrupt it. The "Pits" section of the site lists members who have been banned from the community; right there, like a bulletin board in a public square, are the handles of

171 people. The site even does the math: the banned members represent "0.054% of all users" since the site's founding.

BMW pays attention to this forum. Considering Mullet's strong marketing skills, it's smart of the company. In July 2006 it invited him and 79 journalists to test-drive the 2007 Mini, but Mullet kept the news from his community. After his secret test-drive experience, Mullett launched his own marketing campaign for unveiling the new model to his community. He posted a banner ad in the community: "27.07.2006—MINI2," with no other explanation. For two weeks, members speculated about its meaning. In the hour before the announcement, the community was buzzing with excitement. Members from around the world reported sitting in front of their computers, snacks and beverages nearby, waiting for the announcement. At midnight and every five minutes thereafter, Mullet became a Mini marketer, posting an insider's peek at the 2007 edition. He had detailed reviews of every new feature in the car. He posted close-up photos and videos of the interior and exterior. He posted videos of him test-driving the car on an off-track course. Community members were ecstatic. Some were so taken they said it clinched their decision to buy the 2007 model.

4.

Firecrackers are the one-hit wonders of citizen marketers.

Sometimes the proverbial wild hair springs up and a few friends create a funny homemade video in 20 minutes, post it to a video-sharing site, and watch it accumulate tens of thousands of views. Not all Firecrackers are get-'em-out-fast productions. George Masters's iPod ad was a one-hit wonder, but he spent five months creating it. Firecrackers typically attract considerable attention because they have created a song, animation, video, or novelty that generates a lot of interest but tends to die out quickly as the creators go on with their other work. But the Firecrackers illustrate three principles of amateur content in the social media universe: (1) memes, even latent ones, can live indefinitely on the Web (memes are discussed more fully in chapter 6); (2) social media networks accelerate the spread of memes; and (3) people love to mimic what entertains them.

Take the song "Milk and Cereal." If you listen to this song, it will probably stick in your mind. It burrows deep into the auditory cortex and doesn't leave. "Milk and Cereal" is a pseudonovelty kids' song and describes the joys of various cereals: "In the morning/At your table/Milk and cereal/No Grape-Nuts for grandma." The chorus repeats "milk and cereal" over and over. The lyrics include the taglines for familiar cereals: "Trix are for kids"; "*A* is for apple, *J* is for Jack"; and "Cuckoo for Cocoa Puffs"; to name a few.

The Philadelphia-based group G. Love & Special Sauce wrote and recorded the song but never released it. In 2003 two Virginia Tech students—Dan Loveless and Matt Feidler—got their hands on it and filmed themselves in front of a webcam lip-synching to it. Their production values are unabashedly amateur. Spoons double as microphones. A box of Apple Cinnamon Cheerios and a jug of milk figure prominently. The two guys pop up and down behind the cereal and milk like characters in a Whack-a-Mole arcade game. It's pretty goofy. "It was just a spontaneous idea to do something with ten minutes of our free time," Feidler said. Then they posted a link to the video on the Web. "We put it in our instant-message profiles and didn't tell anyone," he said. That, they figured, would be the end of their goofy video.

Friends with instant-message profiles watched the video and started passing the link around to other friends. Those friends sent it to their friends, and pretty soon it was, as some call it, a "viral video." It spread from person to person. By late 2005, almost two years later, parodies of their video started popping up on video-sharing Web sites. An "Asian response" video by two Stanford University students of Asian descent was popular; it had more than 100,000 views on one video-sharing Web site. By June 2006, fans had created more than 200 parodies and copycat versions, including an Asian girl version, black version, clay-animation version, white boys version, Indian version, Scottish version, German version, Brazilian version, and a green version, starring Yoda and Sasquatch. (The version descriptions come from the video makers themselves, not us.)

G. Love & Special Sauce's song has been heard by hundreds of thousands of people thanks to the copycats. Several cereals have had starring roles, too: Post's Honey Bunches of Oats, Fruity Pebbles, and Raisin Bran. But Cheerios was clearly the star of most copycats. Some videos were watched more than others, a by-product of on-screen talent. But the work of amateurs commonly fuels buzz among online social networks. A professionally created video designed to look amateur usually looks exactly like that. For the short time that Feidler and Loveless spent creating their video, they have reaped a few rewards: an entry in Wikipedia. A mention in the *New York Times*. Then an e-mail arrived from G. Love, who wanted the guys to create a compilation video of the copycats for a future project.

In the first, formative years of social media, the work of Feidler and Loveless sits in early contrast to the rumored $4 million Kraft paid to have its Post Grape-Nuts Trail Mix Crunch featured in a contrived episode of the television series *The Apprentice*. The breakfast cereal had a starring appearance on the television show based on a deal that required four months of work and involved three companies, including *TV Guide*, which engineered the agreement and helped shape subsequent traditional media and marketing promotions. *TV Guide's* publisher is quoted as saying that product placements "drive viewership and constantly reinforce the products' message in concert with the shows." Product placement on television shows has become a popular form of product promotion, and the *Apprentice* episode showed the cereal's brand managers carefully stage-managing the characters on the show. But Kraft's $4 million investment may have been for naught. Based on data from Information Resources, Inc. (a company that tracks the sale of grocery products), in the two months prior to the episode's airing, Kraft was selling about $2.7 million of Grape-Nuts Trail Mix Crunch each month. For the month after the show's airing, sales increased about $600,000, to $3.3 million. But for the five subsequent months, sales dropped to an average of $2.1 million per month. The show apparently gave the cereal a momentary bump in sales, but then tapered off quickly. The cereal was actually selling better before the show. As the audiences for video-sharing sites grow quickly, they threaten to equal or surpass the reach of traditional broadcast networks, putting the future of million-dollar product-placement deals into question. Amateur videos like "Milk and Cereal" demonstrate that the new intersection of technology, pop culture, and marketing make some product placements authentic, buzzworthy, and free.

Even though they may disappear as quickly as they arrived, the Firecrackers can have a measurable impact on a slice of culture or business. One day, a 17-year-old girl who goes by the online handle "Bowiechick" (her real name is Melody Oliveria) wrote a diary post. In the early years of the 21st century, a personal diary for some teens is to sit at the computer, turn on a $99 video camera, record your innermost thoughts, and post them on the Internet. Bowiechick is one of those teens, and she posts her work to the video-sharing site *YouTube.com*. On one particular day in 2005, while talking about the troubles of young love, she also covered her face in cat whiskers, a mustache, a gas mask, and funky hats, all of which were created digitally. The effects were cartoonish but precisely placed along the contours of her face, creating an instant sense of wow! Thousands of links to her post flourished, creating waves of word of mouth. About 1.2 million people watched her video. Hundreds left comments on her post, many of them questions about the effects. The Bowiechick video illustrates two fundamental principles about social media, especially with amateur culture: social media simplifies word of mouth and facilitates collaboration. Bowiechick wasn't video blogging in obscurity—the thousands of links and hundreds of comments on her post are immediately available to her or anyone else who blogs. It's a real-time feedback system on one's ability to strike a chord within culture. Because of the feedback, Bowiechick created another video a few days later explaining how she had created the effects. Simple, actually. Software included with her Logitech computer webcam made the effects easy, like a mouse click.

Bowiechick's response video illustrates a culture of collaboration taking root with social media. The future of personal publishing and the business of culture are being driven by the inherent ease and desire for people to build knowledge together. The academic world has done this for eons, building knowledge atop one another's research and relying on a peer-review process to validate work. The amateur culture attempts something similar, but the time period is days or hours. Validation is from in-bound links. Some 250,000 views later of her explanatory video, Bowiechick helped fuel a spike in sales of the webcam on *Amazon.com*. From *Amazon.com* Logitech learned that sales of the QuickCam Orbit, the product showcased in the video, increased by 128 percent over the same time frame from the previous year. Logitech was awaking to the future of amateur culture, too. Several months later, it formed a partnership with YouTube to make posting videos created by its camera and software to the video-sharing site virtually seamless.

Firecrackers can invite unwanted attention, too. Vincent Ferrari, a 30-year-old New Yorker from the Bronx, had heard "horror stories" of people trying to cancel their accounts with AOL. When he decided to cancel his account, he recorded the call to help prove the stories right or wrong. His 21-minute recording featured an AOL representative doggedly trying to convince an unmovable Ferrari to keep his account, at one point asking to speak to his father. With some measure of retribution, Ferrari posted the recording to his blog (AOL later verified its authenticity). It went off like a pack of firecrackers across the Web and made AOL a villain for a week in all manner of what's considered American media. "This is my way of fighting back. The big company can't trample on the little guy anymore," he told ABC's *Nightline* in a segment for the news show. If anything, the experience of Ferrari cast a new light on call-center tactics. ABC called it "the revenge of the consumers."

Whether it's the creative whims of videographers or the revenge of the consumers, social media is making it easier and faster to spread news. Reputations are enhanced or pummeled at faster and, to some, alarming rates. The work of citizen marketers is a stunning reflection of the democratic principle of freedom of expression. Their use of social media tools in the context of democracy is clearly "We, the people." When the people talk, it's time to listen. Not because of what they say, but because of who they represent.

The work of citizen marketers is typically defined by three commonalities:

1. Personal expression. Their opinions or their journalism are their own, designed to inform, entertain, or analyze in a way that builds a case. It's not unlike what a professional journalist, pundit, or analyst would do.

2. Amateur status. The citizen marketers are usually volunteers and don't announce their arrival with the noisy banging of pots and pans of an expensive marketing program. They are transparent about their motives and associations.

They must be, for the amateur detectives in the blogosphere will undoubtedly sniff them out and expose them.

3. Freely given. Their work is not meant to steal money, time, or attention away from the company of their affiliation. It's meant to enhance or improve it. Their work is a contribution to the commons.

The citizen marketers of the world are adapting to their simultaneous roles of publisher, distributor, and syndicator. They are accelerating changes in traditional media structures, and they are spawning new forms of democratic and participatory collaboration. They're learning that *what* is said is as important as *who* says it and *where* it is said. They're making authenticity and transparency their founding, democratic principles and using their considerable organizing abilities to inspire the democratization of content, processes, and marketing. They are democratizing engagement.

Chances are you can sing the commercial jingle "Oh, I wish I were an Oscar Mayer wiener" right now and recall its melody and most of its words. That 30-second song has aired continuously in 19 countries since 1963, making it the second-longest-running jingle in American history. (The longest-running commercial jingle is from Chiquita Bananas: "I'm Chiquita Banana, and I've come to say, bananas have to ripen in a certain way.")

The cultural roots of the Oscar Mayer wiener jingle extend all the way down, or up, to symphony orchestras, which play it regularly. The wiener jingle permeated our cultural psyche thanks to repeated playing on the powerful megaphones of radio and television. In a twist of irony, the Oscar Mayer wiener jingle wasn't the work of a creative team at J. Walter Thompson, Mayer's advertising agency at the time. It was written by Richard Trentlage. He'd entered a tape of his song—sung by his son and daughter, who had a head cold at the time—into a contest the company had created. When he heard it, Oscar G. Mayer, the company's president at the time, loved it.

"It's wonderful," Mayer told Trentlage and a passel of ad agency executives. "You made that little girl sound like she has a cold."

Of course, she actually had a cold. Anything other than reality would have sounded contrived. The authenticity resonated with Mayer: "Every mother has a daughter who has sounded like that." The simplicity and catchiness of the jingle stunned radio-station music directors when listeners called, asking them to play the jingle as if it were a hit song. That helped sell a lot of hot dogs. All of which leads us to a guiding principle of citizen-created content: people are the antidote to the manufactured reality injected into culture every day.

People are the message.

People are the message when people say "word of mouth" is the most influential form of media on their decision making. Research firm BIGresearch polled 15,000 people and asked them to rate the influence of media on their decision making. Word of mouth was number one.

People are the message when the excessive number of advertising messages creates demand for products to block them. In a 2005 survey, Yankelovich Inc. discovered that 69 percent of Americans would pay for products that block out marketing and advertising. They also found that more than half of Americans avoid buying anything from a company that overwhelms them with advertising. The message Americans are trying to send the message saturators is cool it. Yet the saturators carry on, spurring the growth of an industry focused on shutting the advertisers out.

People are the message when their intent is authentic. Bowiechick was an authentic citizen marketer, not an agent in a program with instructions to spread buzz. As a Firecracker, her authentic product placement on a powerful distribution platform caused a notable surge in camera sales. Bowiechick was the message, not the messenger. That's an important distinction for marketers fixated on *using* people to deliver messages. The world of citizen content creators is largely governed by a universal law of authenticity. Bowiechick's medium happened to be YouTube, a star among video-sharing Web sites where millions of people watch hundreds of millions of videos every day. With democratic authority, viewers determine popularity and relevance. Bowiechick is a sincere and quirky video blogger. She's a high school student, not a paid actor. That made her random webcam demonstration credible. Logitech just happened to be a rather surprised but pleased benefactor. If Logitech had tried to engineer a product placement with Bowiechick or any of the other amateurs who use video blogging as a medium of their self-expression, it would have backfired. Faking authenticity is a difficult art. Just ask any actor.

People are the message when they have roots of credibility. When a blog claimed to have found a French fry in the shape of Abraham Lincoln's head, it was quickly flagged as a fake blog, designed to piggyback to the advertising campaign McDonald's had run with the 2005 Super Bowl. Someone connected with McDonald's had tried to manufacture buzz; the stunt backfired as hundreds of bloggers wrote scathing critiques of the French fry blog, its lack of history, or any identifiable information about the writers. All were obvious tip-offs.

The citizen marketers we identified and spoke with didn't always resemble each other in age, life experiences, or demographic profiles. Some have built sizable followings with their work. They interact with readers and viewers. They publicly live parts of their lives online; because of that, they sometimes endure withering criticism and scrutiny. ("Yuck. I would break up with you just because you're nasty," wrote one impolite viewer of Bowiechick's video.) Citizen marketers are transparent about their motivations and interests—commonsense virtues, certainly, but important to establishing and maintaining credibility. It could be argued that transparency among online-content creators is the result of overwhelming social pressure online to disclose actual or perceived conflicts of interest. A good deal of skepticism often bordering on cynicism pervades some social networks; the magicians of credibility will always try to take advantage of a trusting public to trick it into believing something that isn't real.

One outward goal of many citizen marketers is to build a relationship with the company. For instance, Mike Kaltschnee posted to his blog an e-mail exchange with a Netflix public-relations employee. In it, he asked the company to answer questions submitted by his readers that weren't covered by the company's own frequently asked questions page on its Web site. "I promise to keep this friendly (I do like you guys)," he wrote. The PR representative responded but may as well not have, given the ire he raised among the HackingNetflix readership and dozens of other bloggers: "We appreciate your interest in Netflix, but we must decline your request at this time." Some marketing and public-relations bloggers publicly criticized Netflix for its cold-shoulder treatment of Kaltschnee. "A perfect example of how poorly many companies understand the opportunities of weblogs," wrote Rick Bruner on the Business Blog Consulting site.

"PR pros, please try to keep in mind that oftentimes bloggers can be your greatest ally. They are powerful customer evangelists who often want to help you drive awareness. . . . Unfortunately, Netflix doesn't seem to get this," wrote Steve Rubel, a senior executive at the PR firm Edelman, on his personal blog Micro Persuasion.

Kaltschnee's response on his blog is instructive for any organization hoping to stay in the good graces of bloggers and reduce the risk of bad buzz pinging across the Internet:

> When I worked in public relations, I tried hard to answer every phone or e-mail request, no matter how small the publication. I spoke at user groups at every opportunity (and public speaking used to make me physically ill!). It's hard to get companies to take bloggers seriously. I really like Netflix, but they are slowly withdrawing, closing themselves off from their customers. Instead, companies should be embracing these online communities, comprised mostly of the highly desired "early adopters" that evangelize products to the general population.

The work of citizen marketers may be considered on the fringes of culture and personal expression when compared to what the majority of people create on the Web, but their work hardly goes unnoticed. As we have seen thus far, some work produced by citizen marketers can find large audiences. But an audience needn't be large to be influential. When messages are influential, it is because they are authentic. When they are created and delivered beyond the boundaries of corporate marketing mechanisms, messages are more authentic. That's the value and promise of word of mouth; authenticity contributes to authority. A distinct advantage citizen marketers hold over many traditional media is what we call *dynamic authority*. It is authority fueled by continuous, productive activity. Mike Kaltschnee has dynamic authority. He quickly created a name for himself as an authority on Netflix because of his intense focus on it and his ongoing interaction with readers. His frequent blog posts, forcefulness of purpose, and consistent interaction with his audience leads to dynamic authority.

Although Netflix did respond to his inquiry, the company demonstrated little dynamic authority when it gave Kaltschnee the brush-off (in fact, research by one company found that nearly half of all North American businesses never reply to e-mail inquiries at all). Traditional media can be authoritative, certainly, but its authority is often static. A message may appear in the *Economist, Harper's,* or the *South China Morning Post* in the form of an ad or a story about a brand, product, or organization, but those media are not engineered to respond to the guffaws, objections, or questions of readers in a timely fashion, if at all. All three publications are excellent sources of information and news, but they are still bound by the institutional expectations of one-way media. That's why students of marketing, the discipline most often responsible for distributing an organization's message, are taught the AIDA model: get Attention, hold Interest, arouse Desire, and obtain Action. If substantive questions or concerns generated by traditional media go unanswered, or the message is odious or too obtuse to understand, there is little hope of moving toward action. One-way media creates a static authority. One-way media avoids interaction, engagement, and conversation.

With citizen-created content, people are the message because their role as publishers or broadcasters hoists them above the boundaries that one-way media communicators have erected around themselves. Citizen marketers and online-content creators with substantial audiences and dynamic authority rely upon and thus interact with their audiences. They work in the public piazzas where other people write, work, and play, too. They are not the balcony standers of one-way media, concealed behind walls of organizational privacy. Participation is their medium and their platform.

CHAPTER TWO

The 1 Percenters

*We're the 1 percenters, man—the 1 percent that don't fit and
don't care. So don't talk to me about your doctor bills and your traffic
warrants—I mean you get your woman and your bike and your
banjo and I mean you're on your way. We've punched our way
out of a hundred rumbles, stayed alive with our boots and fists.
We're royalty among motorcycle outlaws, baby.*

A Hell's Angel, speaking for the permanent record,
as quoted in *Hell's Angels,* by Hunter S. Thompson

As a patch, it's pretty simple: a diamond shape surrounded by
a blue border, with "1%" embroidered in the middle. It's worn
over the heart by members of motorcycle clubs that celebrate their
outlaw status from mainstream motorcycle society. They call
themselves the "1 Percenters."

The inspiration for the patch and its meaning can be traced to
1947, when members of the Pissed Off Bastards of Bloomington
Motorcycle Club and the Boozefighters Motorcycle Club showed
up in Hollister, California, for that town's annual motorcycle race.
As sometimes happens with parties involving beer in summer
heat, things got out of hand. A photographer for *Life* magazine
happened to be attending the race and snapped a picture of a
drunken biker perched atop a Harley-Davidson and surrounded
by broken beer bottles. *Life* published the photo with this caption:
"Cyclist's holiday: he and friends terrorize town." A brief story

accompanying the photo said 4,000 members of a motorcycle club caused destructive mayhem in Hollister. That, the story goes, provoked the American Motorcyclists Association to denounce the boozed-up bikers. It assured a worried public that 99 percent of its members were law-abiding citizens, thereby marginalizing the remaining "1 percent" as outlaws.

The story has been the inspiration and founding principle for outlaw motorcycle clubs around the world. One Percenters organize and wear their patches as the proverbial finger raised toward society's expectations of them. The 1954 movie *The Wild Ones,* starring Marlon Brando as the disaffected leader of a motorcycle gang that "terrorizes" a town for a weekend (well, just its fuddy-duddies), helped propel the legend of the 1 Percenters, too. For decades, the story of what happened in Hollister has been repeated by numerous writers in magazines and newspapers, codifying its legend. William L. Dulaney spent months researching the story and the motorcycle culture for the scholarly periodical *The International Journal of Motorcycle Studies.* He argues that "outlaw" motorcycle gangs are not necessarily procriminal; rather, they are antibureaucracy. Although a few clubs have problems with drugs and the law, they are "the vast minority." Nor do the clubs live to break the law. They are organized around the idea of a community, and their unconventional lives and motorcycle lifestyles are reinforced by the strong-as-steel bonds with other members. They revel, sometimes raucously and in beer-soaked pandemonium, in a culture that conventional society frowns on. Forget seeking the approval of conventional governing bodies; the 1 Percenters revel in their minority status. They are outlaws of culture.

Dulaney surprises us, though, by debunking several facts about Hollister. The photo of the drunken biker? The *Life* photographer staged it. There was rowdiness in the town on that fateful weekend, but police made only one arrest. And there's no evidence the American Motorcyclists Association denounced the rowdy bikers either, 1 percent or otherwise. The legend of the 1 Percenters arose from a motorcycling magazine editor who chastised *Life* for its Hollister coverage: "We regretfully acknowledge there was disorder in Hollister—not the acts of 4,000 motorcyclists, but rather of a small percentage of that number."

Even if the facts about Hollister were off, it illustrates the power of an enduring myth and a premise that resonated with a slice of American culture. A 1 Percenter patch became "a badge of social status," as Dulaney surmises, a badge that lives on in a number of American motorcyclist communities today.

The 1 Percenters is an apt analogy to describe citizen marketers. They, too, are outlaws of culture. What they do is well beyond the norm, but with innate talent and a lot of passion, citizen marketers are building considerable audiences. Like the outlaw motorcycle clubs, citizen marketers usually work outside the boundaries of a corporation or sanctioning body. Sometimes there is little recognition for it, but they are dedicated to and protective of their work and the community they create. They excel on the edges of culture even if their percentage as content creators is little more than a statistical error to some companies. They are not a huge number, but that's not the point.

Take, for instance, Wikipedia—a Web-based encyclopedia that, just like *Encyclopaedia Britannica,* strives to keep a neutral point of view about its numerous subjects. Unlike *Britannica,* which was first published in 1768 and is often considered the foremost authority on a topic, anyone who visits *Wikipedia.org* can contribute to it. In June 2005, 7.4 million people visited Wikipedia. That's a big number, equivalent to the population of New York

City. While 7.4 million people had the egalitarian and democratic opportunity to add new content or make changes to Wikipedia, only 68,682 people did. That's 0.9 percent of visitors. Since Wikipedia's inception in 2001, the percentage of visitors who have created content for it has always been about 1 percent, plus or minus several tenths of a point. Moreover, in the first five years of Wikipedia's history, 1.8 percent of the site's visitors have written more than 72 percent of all articles. That means by June 2006, with the article count up to 1.2 million and its traffic having surged to a staggering 25 million visitors per month, Wikipedia's 1 Percenters had written 864,000 articles. A fraction of its total visitors were largely responsible for creating content that made it one of the 20 most-visited Web sites in the world. By comparison, the 2006 edition of *Encyclopaedia Britannica,* which relies on subject-matter experts for its content, had just over 100,000 articles.

Other online communities dependent upon the work of contributors share similar data about participation rates, and they share a similar characteristic: a tiny percentage of their visitors contribute content. Based on our research into the work of citizen marketers, we postulate *the 1% Rule.* The rule is simple: About 1 percent of the total number of visitors to a democratized forum will create content for it or contribute content to it. Furthermore, we postulate that about 10 percent of the total number of visitors will interact with the contributed content. *Interact* may be described as writing comments or voting on content items. But the 1% Rule is the guiding principle. The rule is not absolute— it's an estimate based on our research—and we encourage community creators to set contribution goals and expectations beyond it. One percent is a low figure, perhaps lower than what many people would expect, hope, or plan on, but based on what we've seen among a sample set of Web sites, it's roughly the norm, give or take a few points. We established the 1% Rule by using existing data that's publicly available and requesting data from a number of communities that rely on volunteers to create content.

One example of the 1% Rule can be found with Yahoo Groups, a free service from Yahoo that allows anyone to create an online community for just about anything. About 9.2 million people visit Yahoo Groups each month, but only about 1 percent of them are content originators, according to one of the company's technology chiefs. Of Yahoo Groups' total visitors, about "1 percent of the user population might start a group or a thread within a group," according to Bradley Horowitz, the company's vice president of product strategy. After that, about 10 percent of the total audience of any Yahoo Group interacts with citizen content or, in his words, "synthesizes" it. Horowitz is quick to point out that the upshot in this scenario is that creators and synthesizers "provide value for 100 percent of the total audience." The other benefit is that Yahoo gets content-rich sites created by uncompensated workers for which it can sell highly targeted, niche advertising.

QuickBooks Community is an online forum designed to help the 4 million customers of Intuit's accounting software help one another answer questions about the product and solve one another's accounting challenges. In July 2006, the QuickBooks Community hosted 100,000 visitors, and 900 of them created new content threads on the site. Those 900 people represented 0.9 percent of its total visitors, according to data the company shared with us.

The TiVo Community Forum (*TiVoCommunity.com*), dedicated to the digital video recorder, is independent of the company and run by a citizen marketer. Tens of thousands of customers and fans of TiVo spend time every day at the site. TiVo Community Forum founder David Bott says about 1.1 million people visit the site every month. Based on data he shared with us, we estimate that less than 0.3 percent of all site visitors start new a discussion thread each month.

ProductWiki.com is similar to Wikipedia in that it relies on a community of volunteers to create content for its encyclopedic catalog. Its visitors, however, write neutral product descriptions or reviews, all designed to appeal to people researching a decision to buy something. Like Wikipedia, ProductWiki allows anyone to create an entry about an existing product or edit an existing entry. The site debuted in late 2005 and has grown quickly; its total visitor count grows about 30 percent every month. In July 2006, 75,901 people visited ProductWiki, and 188 of those visitors contributed content to it. That means 0.2 percent of the visitors wrote an entry or edited an existing one. Data for April, May, and June of 2006 show similar percentages of contributors even though the total number of visitors was markedly different each month. When Erik Kalviainen, one of the site's founders, tallied all of the writing and editing, commenting, and "tapping"—a voting tool that allows visitors to vote for a product they'd like to buy—the contributor rate rises to 3.6 percent for July 2006. That percentage is the average for the three previous months as well.

Channel 9 (*channel9.msdn.com*) is a community Web site developed by Microsoft for programmers who develop applications using Microsoft's various technologies. Community visitors create most of the content for the site, including online forum posts, wiki pages and photos. For our research, one of Channel 9's founders compiled data about the site and found that in June 2006, 4.5 million people visited Channel 9 and 11,420 of them created new content for it. That is less than 0.2 percent of total visitors.

Discovery Education, a unit of Discovery Communications, launched a Web site in 2005 for teachers who instruct children from kindergarten through high school. The Discovery Educator Network invites teachers to connect with one another and share their experiences and knowledge about digital media tools in the classroom. (We helped Discovery design the program; for more on

DEN, see Chapter 7.) It reports slightly higher percentages of con-tributors. In July 2006, 9,877 people visited the site, and 422 of them, or 4.3 percent, created content for it. Steve Dembo is the DEN's community manager, and he theorizes that "unlike most online communities, we have 20 managers who are spending 80 percent of their time in face-to-face events with people teaching them how to use the site and encouraging them to do so." Plus, the site has created an incentive plan to encourage content contributions: to gain access to some of the site's other features, a member must submit a piece of content such as a lesson plan.

Sites with contributor percentages substantially better than 1 percent would be noteworthy; considering the secrecy with which many commercial operations guard their Web site data, it's difficult to determine vast exceptions to the rule. For content creation in the age of social media and amateur culture, the 1% Rule may subvert the well-established 80/20 rule, a guiding rule of thumb for millions of managers around the world. The 80/20 rule posits that 20 percent of something is typically responsible for 80 percent of the results. The 80/20 rule was popularized by Joseph Juran, an industrial engineer who grew into prominence as a quality guru and management theorist. In 1941, when he discovered the work of economist Vilfredo Pareto, he was struck by Pareto's observation that 20 percent of the residents in Italy owned 80 percent of the wealth. Juran expanded Pareto's work, calling it the Pareto Principle, and applied it to the management of people and things in business. He called it the "vital few" versus the "trivial many" (later amended to the "useful many"), and it has been a guiding business principle ever since.

The 1% Rule (as well as the Pareto Principle) can be explained by what scientists call a power law. It is used to explain a variety of phenomenon, like the most commonly used words, the occurrence of names in most cultures, the sales of books, the sales of movie tickets, annual incomes, the sizes of earthquakes—anything where phenomena tend to be highly concentrated. Power laws also explain how a small number of Web sites can generate significant levels of traffic. If you were to add up the number of people who visit Yahoo, MySpace, YouTube, Wikipedia, and Digg, their combined traffic would dwarf the combined traffic of tens of thousands of randomly chosen Web sites. Power laws explain why only a small number of people write most of the articles on Wikipedia even though millions of people can. Clay Shirky, who teaches new media at New York University, explained power laws in 2003, when blogs were beginning to appear with increasing frequency: "A new social system starts and seems delightfully free of the elitism and cliquishness of the existing systems. Then, as the new system grows, problems of scale set in. Not everyone can participate in every conversation. Not everyone gets to be heard. Some core group seems more connected than the rest of us. What matters is this: diversity plus freedom of choice creates inequality, and the greater the diversity, the more extreme the inequality."

Not everyone will take up the offer to participate in a contest, create content, or leave a comment. In fact, the odds are that very few will. Power laws tell us that distribution of action is uneven across a widespread field of play. The vast majority of people involved will be spectators, happily munching their popcorn, observing for a bit and then moving on. It may be tempting to call the observers freeloaders, but that would be a misnomer. Something attracted them to the field, and their possibility as a future content creator, synthesizer, or connector to other networks is a real possibility. But with power laws and the 1% Rule, inequality is the rule, not the exception. This means that building a solid core of early adopting volunteers or contributors is critical to creating a successful community-driven Web site or to launching a new product or designing a grassroots campaign. In the AIDA model we described in Chapter 1 (get attention, hold interest, arouse desire, and obtain action), the 1 Percenters help lead others to action.

Although we don't consider the people who contribute to Wikipedia, Digg, and other sites relying on amateur content as citizen marketers (they're more apt to be called 1 Percenters), they share many commonalities; *Boston Globe* reporter David Mehegan found the contributors are generally in their 20s and computer savvy. "They are highly educated, intellectually curious, sociable, interested in many things and in finding new interests," according to Mehegan. "They are accustomed to the world of Google, blogs, user groups, meetups, instant messaging, and free and open information on the Internet." More are men than women. From a motivation standpoint, they are idealistic about free information but not blind to its challenges. "It might not be reliable, but I know that people are generally [contributing] because they want to provide accurate information," states Branford Stafford, describing his role as a Wikipedia contributor. "They're not getting anything out of it—no money. I don't think disseminating false information is satisfying to people, but distributing useful information is." Distributing false information is useful to some people, especially during political elections, but the collectivism of Wikipedia compels its contributors to actively patrol for disinformation as well.

Indeed, vandalism is one of Wikipedia's challenges as an open book, and it may also be a challenge to the creators of democratized forums. One high-profile case of digital vandalism within Wikipedia was at the expense of one-time political figure and newspaper publisher John Seigenthaler. With five sentences that insinuated a role in the Kennedy assassinations, a vandal defamed the respected Seigenthaler, and the sentences went unnoticed for four months until they were brought to the retired publisher's attention. After informing Wikipedia cofounder Jimmy Wales of the content,

Seigenthaler wrote a scathing editorial in *USA Today* in which he called Wikipedia "a flawed and irresponsible research tool." Several days later, a volunteer sleuth unmasked the anonymous vandal by tracing his computer footprint, which Wikipedia had captured. A Tennessee man had added the fake data as a joke to shock a co-worker who knew the Seigenthaler family. He apologized and the matter was dropped.

Another challenge is dealing with wipeout vandals—people who eliminate entire chunks of content. That form of vandalism typically focuses on a small number of well-known people where a neutral point of view is difficult, such as George W. Bush and, oddly, the singer Christina Aguilera. Wikipedia contributors are not required to have credentialed authority for the articles they write, and until the Seigenthaler incident, they were not required to cite the sources of their information. But Wikipedia has changed some of its practices, including "protecting" a handful of the site's most frequently vandalized subjects from being edited by the masses. Some bloggers have criticized Wikipedia's content moderation as a sign of failure or even the "death" of democratized publishing models. But the idea that any Web site designed as an experiment in democratic participation can't undergo changes or modifications without signifying its death is profoundly preten-tious. Even the U.S. Constitution, the paragon of institutional-ized democracy idealized, has 27 amendments. While Wikipedia's openness may make it more vulnerable to vandals and criticism, early indications are that content created by its contributors is pretty accurate. The scientific journal *Nature* found that Wikipedia is about as accurate as *Britannica* when comparing articles from both sites; of eight "serious errors" the journal's reviewers found, four came from each source.

Will the 1% Rule doom plans to dedicate resources toward democratized communities if only a small percentage of people are going to create content for them? In some cases, that may be a prudent decision. The 1% Rule could be considered a rule of thumb in developing baseline expectations for content creation. Investing in elaborate participatory sites or expensive tools based on a premise that more than half of visitors will interact with them may be cause for review. Will the 1% Rule mean that content creators are not a representative sample of the existing customer or member population? Most likely. As the experience with the aforementioned sites seems to indicate, 1 Percenters are typically well-educated, highly involved, and on the leading edges of technology. They are not average. They are, like the motorcycle club outlaws, on the fringes of culture. The 1 Percenters contribute toward what they see as a common good even if they are not paid. They invest in the future. They plant the seeds of interaction as a totem of their commitment to the community. They are self-sustaining, and most of all, they are volunteers. That does not seem to prevent them from devoting significant amounts of time, thought, and energy to their work.

How many citizen creators are online? The nonprofit, nonpartisan Pew Internet & American Life Project has sought to answer that question. Every year, it surveys a representative sample of Americans about their use of the Internet. In March 2006, Pew said 48 million Americans were blogging or creating art or video content to post on the Web. *Forty-eight million American content creators.* That's more Web-based content creators than there are people in all of Canada. Forty-eight million is roughly equal to the population of South Korea. Forty-eight million is 35 percent of all Americans who use the Internet. At the growth rate Pew is charting, it might not be long before 100 million Americans are active content creators.

For organizations with business interests in the United States, the idea that even 1 percent of 100 million people—1 million people—could create their own ads, their own marketing campaigns, and their own brand-specific communities without official permission, input, or control is either astoundingly cool or somewhat alarming.

Not all of the citizen creators will have sizable audiences, influence, or (to be fair) a lot of natural talent, but many of them will work hard at developing all three. They will put their reputations on the line because in this new paradigm of message creation and delivery, the citizen marketers *are* the message. It is their unaffiliated, uncompensated work on behalf of a product, brand, company, or person that bolsters their credibility and, therefore, their message. George Masters and Jeff Jarvis created a stir because they arrived at a big-bang point, when a new world of citizen media was brewing in the gaseous chambers of the digital universe. It was also during this time, in November 2004, when another site was born that would help democratize the popularity of stories on the Web: Digg.

Digg.com aggregates stories. Its hundreds of thousands of registered members troll the Internet each day, reading news stories, perusing blogs, or watching videos, then nominate items they believe will be of interest to the larger Digg community. Any of Digg's readers can vote (or *digg*, in their parlance) thumbs up or thumbs down on every submitted item. A real-time tally system determines which items should move up in the queue of popular stories.

Digg was one of the first Web sites to democratize what could be called story hierarchy. When you pick up a copy of the *New York Times* or the *Contra Costa Times,* a small group of editors behind the scenes has determined which stories will appear on their respective front pages. The editors determine the hierarchy of news. It's the same principle for listening to news on NPR or watching CNN: the first story broadcast is typically the most important. But Digg turns that model upside down. Readers determine story hierarchy, especially the ones that will reach its coveted front page. Digg's members are Filters, but in a considerably broader format.

In some circles, the people who nominate stories for sites like Digg (or variants of it, like *Reddit.com* or *Del.icio.us*) are called social bookmarkers. They "bookmark" a story for the benefit of the community. At Digg, hierarchy is determined by a secret formula of four elements: total votes, the relative authority of the nominators, comments from Digg's readers, and the arriving speed of the votes. With votes continually received and tallied, a story may be on Digg's front page for a few hours and then slip off to subsequent pages. (The tally formula is kept secret to prevent gaming of the system.) The number of visitors Digg sends to a site is significant; some sites report a sudden influx of 15,000 new unique visitors in just four days. That's a reflection of the size and curiosity of the Digg community. Digg's democratic principles and ease of use have propelled it to become one of the 25 most popular sites on the Internet. In about 18 months, Digg had registered more 400,000 people as members. Digg grew thanks to a band of 1 Percenters who contributed content.

Here's where the story of Digg, and other online communities in similar situations, takes an interesting twist down an unknown road. Does it make sense to pay 1 Percenters? Even if they are content as volunteers?

Consider an experiment conducted by Jason Calacanis. He is an entrepreneur who sold his blogging company Weblogs Inc. to AOL in 2005 for a reported $25 million. After it bought his company, AOL put Calacanis in charge of *Netscape.com,* one of its news and e-mail portals. He reformulated Netscape as an aggregated news site where, similar to *Digg.com,* visitors determine the ranking of stories on its front page. In July 2006, Calacanis offered to pay "the top 50 users on any of the major social news/bookmarking sites . . . $1,000 a month for your 'social bookmarking' rights. Put in at least 150 stories a month and we'll give you $12,000 a year." (He later amended the offer to the top 12 social bookmarkers.) "Talent wins, and talent needs to get paid," he wrote on his blog. Several weeks later, Calacanis announced that he had hired three contributors from Digg, as well as one contributor each from social bookmarking sites Newsvine and Reddit. The remaining hires were internal candidates from his company Weblogs Inc. He didn't meet his goal of the "top 12 social bookmarkers" from the "major social news/bookmarking sites," and it may take at least one to two years to see how his experiment plays out.

Calacanis's offer was an experiment in the microeconomics of labor. The volunteer cultures at Digg, Wikipedia, Reddit, Del.icio.us, and others would probably baffle Adam Smith, the most famous and perhaps most influential economist of all time. He theorized in 1776 that "we are not ready to suspect any person of being defective in selfishness. . . . It is not from the benevolence of the butcher, the brewer, or the baker that we expect our dinner, but from their regard to their own interest." Smith's influence is still felt today as companies continue to offer cash, points, or rewards in exchange for loyalty or word of mouth. "No man but a blockhead ever wrote, except for money," as Samuel Johnson once wrote. The greatest reward of all is cash, or so the thinking goes. That somewhat sums up the belief system of Smith, Calacanis, and others: talent doesn't, and shouldn't, work for free. This raises two larger questions: (1) since the 1 Percenters are voluntarily producing work on behalf of a commercial operation, and that work increases the value of the operation, should they receive fair compensation like laborers? (2) Who owns this collaborative content—the 1 Percenters, the host organization, or both of them?

For the compensation question, one answer is that they're not laborers. They're *hobbyists*. As hobbyists, they have embraced the principle of the participatory Web. How else to explain the success of commercial online operations, such as Digg, Flickr, Channel 9, YouTube, and others, and the thousands of forums, like TreoCentral, that are volunteer, de facto customer-support sites? These sites prove the viability of what Stanford law professor Lawrence Lessig calls "non-commercial culture" but in the context of commercial culture. The hobbyists are already contributing to a commercial commons without expecting payment or commercial gain.

The 1 Percenters contribute because *it's fun*. Hobbies are supposed to be fun. Hobbies free them from the expectations of labor and deadlines. The 1 Percenters expect only that they and the community improve their skills as hobbyists. So it follows that paying the contributor-hobbyists of a site or community dependent upon citizen content-creators risks converting them into laborers and potentially eliminating the fun. Then it's a job, and not a well-paying one at that; Calacanis's offer of $12,000 per year is slightly below the U.S. poverty level. The median salary of someone who works as a counter attendant at a fast-food restaurant in the United States is $24,000 per year.

For the ownership question, we again turn to professor Lessig: he terms the work produced by citizen marketers and 1 Percenters a contribution to the "read-write culture." As the founder and chairman of the nonprofit Creative Commons organization, Lessig has been an influential force in enabling copyright holders to grant some of their rights to the public while retaining others through a variety of licensing schemes. In the new "read-write culture," he proposes organizations establish interoperable licenses that create equivalent ownership of content that allow people and organizations to freely redistribute it. No one would own the content outright—both parties would—therefore, it is free for others to create content on top of it, or below it. It mirrors the idea of derivative works, minus the granting of copyright. Under copyright law, a derivative work is a creation that includes major portions of someone else's copyrighted work. To use the original work, the second party must seek the permission of the copyright holder. In the read-write culture, seeking permission would present a significantly tall hurdle to cross, and it would virtually bring democratized communities to a crashing halt. Speaking in 2006 at the annual conference for Wikipedia fans, Lessig said, "If we don't solve this problem now, it's an environmental problem we'll be faced with three, five, eight years from now. As islands of creativity, we now have no simple ways of interoperating." The islands of content creation, and ownership, must be united into a freely flowing network.

It's the "network effect" that makes social networks like Digg, Flickr, Reddit, YouTube, MySpace, and others valuable. Just as a telephone is made more valuable by the number of people who also have telephones, so, too, are social-minded networks made more valuable by their growth. As more people join the sites, their value and potential utility grow commensurately. With a potent mix of transparency, participation, and community ownership, all of which are democratic principles tied to citizenship, the sites have grown into specialized communities. Yes, growth introduces more noise to the network, but that's a challenge with every neighborhood, every community. Nonetheless, the organic growth of social networks is based upon a sort of democratic social Darwinism. The interested people stay and form the basis of a community, while the disinterested ones move on.

Is there a model to the economics of human behavior in communities? Gary S. Becker, the Nobel Prize–winning economist, theorizes in *The Economic Approach to Human Behavior* that, at least within families, there is a distinct "unimportance of the distribution of income." That is, not everyone in a family expects a "fair share" of income. "The head's concern about the welfare of other members provides each, including the head, with some insurance against disasters," he writes. In other words, if family members think their leader has their own best interests in mind, they'll sacrifice "distribution of income" because they value the family, especially if it adds to an insurance policy against disasters. This, of course, is dependent on the head of the family not running off to Vegas one day. And remember Michael Marx, who spends part of his free time on the Barqsman blog. When asked why he devotes free time to a blog about a soda, he said, "To keep the brand alive." If we apply Becker's model to the bonds established by community, then we could argue the work of Marx and other citizen marketers is to reduce the risks of worsening product quality, deteriorating customer service, or falling behind competitors. They are contributing to an insurance policy against "disasters."

Paying citizen marketers, citizen content creators, or 1 Percenters overlooks the nature of hobbyism and the family bonding that occurs over time. *Digg.com* launched in December 2004 and took about 18 months to acquire 400,000 registered users and a core community of contributors, all of whom worked for free. Their contributions signify their loyalty, and creating loyalty is a slow, challenging process. Paying a few social bookmarkers among a larger group of them introduces a hierarchy of labor and may well become a disincentive for others to contribute. "It's the users that need the power to moderate, and giving each one of them a slice of the power is the best way to do it," Digg founder Kevin Rose told us. The communities have helped shape their own futures, thereby giving them a sense of ownership, of citizenship. That power is more valuable than cash. One of Digg's top contributors wrote on his blog that he declined Calacanis's offer because "I don't need to be paid what I do now. I will commit my time to Digg whenever possible, that's how much I enjoy Digg. It's not about the money, it's what you enjoy, and this is what I like."

Spending 12 to 18 months creating a community of contributors who believe in the idea, the community, or the Web site and its vision hardly seems like a foolish investment. If content contributors believe in the cause, they'll do the work for free. That's the basis of most volunteer work. Almost all of the citizen marketers we spoke with emphasized their work is a contribution toward a common good in pursuit of a hobby. Paying established social bookmarkers seems like trying to improve product loyalty by buying a Super Bowl commercial: it's a bet, but the odds are against it.

Does the 1% Rule apply to your internal or external Web site? To apply the formula, pick a period of time, such as a month. Take the number of people who create new or original content (x) and divide that by the total number of people who visit the site (y). The resulting percentage (n) is your answer ($n = x \div y$). Keep the 1% Rule in mind for the chapters ahead. As we'll see, the value of contributions made by 1 Percenters and citizen marketers can be measurably strong.

~

By now you may be wondering, why *"citizens"*? Why not just call them consumers? Or users? How about amateurs?

To explain why, let's go back a few thousand years to Athens, Greece. Athenians created the idea of citizenship by ensuring— even expecting—that each one takes responsibility for his or her city-state. It was the birth of democracy, and it's a classic tale of power concentrated too strongly in the hands of the few and how abuse of power eventually led to revolution. In Athens, the balance of power favored landowners over everyone else.

"A few proprietors owned all the soil, and the cultivators with their wives and children were liable to be sold as slaves on failure to pay their rent" or their debts, Aristotle wrote of the times. Since laborers were plentiful, they were paid next to nothing. The lawmaker Draco, a friend to wealthy Athenians, wrote legislation that punished petty theft or simple idleness with death. Draco secured his place in history when we describe lawmakers or authority figures today who enact overly severe or inhumane measures to teach citizens a "lesson."

Economically, Athens was in shambles. Anger and resentment among the lower classes fueled unrest and cultural chaos. With revolution imminent, a number of Athenians called on their respected fellow citizen Solon to take control of the city.

Solon saved Athens from itself by forcing greater levels of equality between rich and poor. He canceled all existing debts owed to individuals or the state. He released anyone who was a slave because of debt, and he freed all those imprisoned by their political beliefs. He legalized and taxed prostitution and established public brothels that were licensed by the state. He set up trials by a jury of peers and established standards for weights and measures. He rescinded the Draconian laws. He established new standards of equality that brought stability and, eventually, prosperity to Athens. Solon meant to break the notion that Athenians were merely assets to be bought and sold—equality should be the deciding factor for governing social behavior, regardless of wealth or status. Solon paved the way for democracy to take root by declining calls to become permanent dictator, saying that dictatorship was "a very fair spot, but there was no way down from it."

Citizenship was born. *Efcharisto!*

Athenians were now in control of their city-state, but it wasn't called *citizenship* then. It was *politeia*. Brook Manville and Josiah Ober have studied the history of citizenship and democracy and explain:

> *Politeia* embraces a richness of meaning whose complexity is exactly the point—implying not just a legal status ("passport-carrying, tax-paying member of a nation"), but a deep and multifaceted sense of civic identity. The word *politeia* encompasses the concepts of "community of citizens," "constitution," "form of government," and even "way of life."

Citizenship was not a political concept. It was the culture of everyday life. When everyday people add to the collective knowledge of a company, product, or brand by creating blog posts, podcasts, or their own product-specific communities, we see that as a way of life. It's their sense of duty contributing toward the common good. Although it may be on behalf of a commercial entity, we're not ones to judge that relative value. After all, free will is a liberating force. For citizen marketers, their work and membership in marketing communities is part of their lives. It's their hobby. It's their *politeia*. It's citizenship in the age of marketing as culture.

CHAPTER THREE

The Democratization
of Everything

For 'tis the sport to have the engineer hoist with his own petard.

From Shakespeare's *Hamlet*

In 1994, Time Warner hatched *Pathfinder.com.*

As the largest entertainment and publishing company in the world and a Fortune 50 company, Time Warner had big plans for its first steps into the new world of the Internet. The company brazenly boasted Pathfinder would become "the world's best Web site" because it would function as the online portal to stories within its stable of famous magazines, like *Time, People, Sports Illustrated, Fortune,* and *Entertainment Weekly* as well as the cable network CNN. Pathfinder was a troubled chick after its hatching because, as one observer at the time wrote, it resembled "an explosion at a Time Warner magazine factory." In the modem-reliant years of 1994–2000, Pathfinder was 100 pounds of gold jewelry on a 3-foot model. It was overloaded with graphics. It bowed under the weight of numerous ads. It was trying to be a glossy print magazine minus the paper. That caused

Pathfinder's front page to load slowly as visitors were forced to travel through the front page to read stories. Over the course of five years, Pathfinder tore through redesigns and sucked up tens of millions of dollars and probably several careers before the company pulled the plug.

What Pathfinder represented was the coming battle for control between the few and the many. Pathfinder was "cumbersome, confusing, and spoke down from the top in a medium that thrived on bubbling up from the bottom," according to writer Kara Swisher. "Like all traditional media companies, it talked while consumers were supposed to listen." Time Warner imposed its gatekeeper role on a medium that rejected hierarchy and control, and the company stubbornly refused to capitulate to the demands of its visitors. Because of its lineage, Pathfinder was a bit like Mary Shelley's fictional monster, a flawed beast of multiple components that could never live a normal life. When the company finally pulled the plug on Pathfinder, a company spokesperson said, "There was more power in the individual brands than the Pathfinder brand. Why bury them under the Pathfinder name? Basically that's what the market told us."

At the same time, two Stanford students, Jerry Yang and David Filo, were building Yahoo. It resembled a public garden more than a castle. Its graphics were simple, and so was its mission: a human-created archive of Internet content. Yahoo's approach relied on egalitarianism and openness, and it stomped Pathfinder in the race for supremacy. Yahoo and its global portals eventually became the most-visited network of Web sites in the world, attracting 500 million visitors per month. Time Warner learned, painfully, that centralized control on the Web is difficult, if not futile.

Such are the forces of democratization. They work incessantly against the forces of control. As the forces of democratization gain strength, they continually compel companies to become more transparent, sometimes against their will. Three separate stories on July 23, 2004, illustrated this concept.

1.

Not long into the 2004 baseball season, parts of Chicago's historic Wrigley Field began to crumble. Literally. Several small yet potentially injurious chunks of concrete plunged into the seats below. One brick-sized chunk landed on a fan's foot during a game. The Cubs made repairs to the storied stadium without telling anyone, including the team's parent, the Tribune Company, which publishes the *Chicago Tribune*. As concrete crumbled, word spread quickly and loudly among Web sites, blogs, and competing media; still, the team said nothing. With the din of buzz now obvious, the *Tribune* and the Cubs finally acknowledged the problem. Cubs president Andy MacPhail asked, during a news conference, "Are we supposed to disclose any time a toilet backs up or we lose a washroom for a couple of innings? I mean, I'm not trying to be facetious, I'm really not. But is that what is required of us?"

Concrete falling into seats is hardly the same as a backed-up washroom, so let's put aside McPhail's questionable comparison for a moment and examine the bigger issue: word of mouth is influence. Since their founding in 1876, the Cubs have benefited from strong relationships with evangelistic, worshipful fans. The team plays to consistently capacity crowds at home, averaging 39,700 fans per game in 2006 in a 41,118-seat stadium. Even though the team is a perennial loser, tickets for Cubs games were the second-most expensive in baseball during 2006, at $34.30 per seat. Word of mouth is a powerful medium because of the trust that's passed from person to person with each message. Waiting weeks to acknowledge what was being said online and off-line, the Cubs simply fueled the questions and speculation. Their hesitancy to acknowledge the obvious was a classic case of information control and, by extension, image control. "Be extremely mysterious, even to the point of soundlessness" is the advice of the Chinese war strategist Sun Tzu, to whom countless managers still listen 2,500 years later. "Thereby you can be the director of the opponent's fate."

                                2.

Control issues startled a small but influential software company whose mission is to democratize personal expression and the spread of information. Six Apart had been in business nearly three years by the summer of 2004. One of its products was Movable Type, software that allows people to create blogs and then communicate easily with people, groups, or the world.

Movable Type is a word-of-mouth success story. The enthusiasm of its earliest supporters fueled the company's organic growth. Then, in July 2004, Six Apart upset hundreds, if not thousands, of those supporters by announcing a dramatic change in its pricing and licensing policy. (Until that point, the software had been largely free, dependent on the donations of its users.) Hundreds of people complained on their blogs about the pricing change. Blogs were designed to make personal expression—no matter its tone—easy and fast, and Six Apart was being swarmed by the potential fury its software could unleash.

Obviously, Six Apart is in charge of its pricing model, but supporters complained that the voice they'd normally had in the company's decision-making process had been ignored. They had taken a stake in the company's success because Six Apart sought their input. That's the deal companies make when relying on the help of customers to grow: customers will volunteer their time and attention, but they will fight for their status and power. Now faced with the loss of status, the bloggers were incensed.

"It wasn't the licensing changes and pricing changes that affected them, it was that we'd sprung it on them," Six Apart cofounder Mena Trott said, after some time had passed. "We're so associated with blogging that people wanted to trust us more. We'd gone from the darlings to being evil. We were more evil than Microsoft." Regaining lost trust is done from a position of weakness, not strength. What eventually helped the company right itself was Trott's candor in acknowledging the complaints and obviousness of the misstep.

3.

Another story on that July day, far beyond the world of business, illustrated the battle between control and transparency. The bipartisan federal commission investigating the 9/11 attacks on the United States released its final report, faulting U.S. intelligence agencies for their systems of secrecy:

> Information was not shared, sometimes inadvertently or because of legal misunderstandings. Analysis was not pooled. Effective operations were not launched. Often the handoffs of information were lost across the divide separating the foreign and domestic agencies of the government . . . [in] symptoms of the government's broader inability to adapt to how it manages problems to the new challenges of the 21st century.

The commission urged Congress to provide greater transparency into the country's intelligence budget. It recommended significantly reducing the amount of classified information and creating a "network-based information-sharing system that transcends traditional governmental boundaries." The commission said excessive secrecy led to "compartmentalization" of records, making it virtually impossible to connect the dots of a deadly plot. Despite the commission's recommendations, the United States continues to retreat from its leadership position in transparent governing. President George W. Bush's administration created 81 percent more secrets in 2005 than in 2000, according to the watchdog coalition *OpentheGovernment.org*. Nearly 70 countries ensure the right to request and review public documents, and many of their laws are more comprehensive and effective than ones in the United States.

Whether at the company, community, or national level, the forces of democratization battle the forces of secrecy in a fight for increased transparency, and social media is giving the upper hand to transparency. The roots of democracy instill in us an expectation of transparent governing by political officials, nonprofits, or appointed company leaders. Leaders in many organizations find themselves facing or making arguments for strong control in the name of protecting formulas, data, plans, or sometimes arrogance versus our everyday expectations of openness. Overbearing forces of secrecy appeal to our fears. The forces of transparency appeal to our hopes and sense of justice.

Time Warner learned that centralized control on the Web is expensive. The Chicago Cubs discovered that word of mouth is being accelerated by Web-based media. Six Apart learned that being open with customers is a virtue for growth but, if taken away for the sake of message control, can be painful and time-consuming. And the 9/11 Commission said the lives of citizens are dependent upon a democracy that remains true to transparency. Free your government, your business, your mind from top-down management. Because control is slipping out of control.

As the World Wide Web celebrated its 13th birthday in 2004, it was beginning to evolve into what some technologists called Web 2.0, the second generation of the Web. For software developers, it's something of a hootenanny term—Web 2.0 can mean different things to different people. We'll define it as *creating collaborative Web experiences when information is shared multilaterally.* If "Web 1.0" was primarily one-way communication between Web-site owner and visitor, then Web 2.0 is multiple-way communication between Web-site owner and visitor, and visitors with other visitors. Web 2.0 has become a mantra for developers who envision openness or as a benchmark for developers who struggle with data-restrictive, control-oriented committees, clients, boards, or bosses. Web 2.0 developers are fueled by the power of XML, a standardized system for describing data that makes it easier to transport data to a browser, cell phone, e-mail program, or any digital device. It is this sharing of data, whether it's through blog posts, podcasts, photos, videos, or maps, that allows it to be *recombined* into new and ever-changing products that stokes the imaginations of some developers.

All of this leads to one tangible, citizen-marketer by-product of Web 2.0 imaginations: mashups. "Mashup" is a Web buzzword to describe a hybrid combination of two or more data sources that when combined, create a new product or improve an existing one. Two of the most prevalent mashups are (1) data mashups and (2) entertainment mashups.

Data mashups are typically created by software developers who often combine the mapping technologies of Yahoo, Google, or MSN (all of which have opened their mapping systems to programmers) with their own data or data that's freely available. For instance, Adrian Holovaty created one of the earliest data mashups by layering crime figures supplied by the Chicago Police Department on top of Google's map system. He wrote a piece of software that automatically visits the police department's Web site each week, scoops up crime data, then sorts it into categories of crime type, street, date, zip code, ward, police district, even commuter train. Every category, every street, and every zip code can be viewed at *ChicagoCrime.org* as a Google Map, with its familiar pushpins of reported crime-scene locations. The audience for his mashup application is virtually unlimited: homeowners, postal carriers, real estate brokers, or police officers, to name a few. This is how Web 2.0 democratizes the future. It creates new products by layering data on top of one another and providing all of the data additional context, meaning, or value.

Holovaty's day job is "editor of editorial innovations" at Washingtonpost.Newsweek Interactive, and he created the mashup and the Web site as a concerned citizen; it's available to anyone, and it depends on his contributions and visitor donations. The Institute for Interactive Journalism awarded ChicagoCrime.org its $10,000 Batten Award in 2005 for innovation in journalism. "It's one journalist's ability to see all the pieces and put them together, but every city should do this as a public service," the judges said in announcing their award.

Software tools like iMovie and GarageBand for the Mac or Microsoft Movie Maker for the PC are bundled with computer purchases. As free yet capable programs, they allow everyday people to play and "remix" videos or songs with other videos and songs and create a new piece of entertainment. Remixing isn't a new idea; hip-hop artists have been remixing songs to create new ones since the 1980s, and that's the story behind mashups—it's a spin-off of hip-hip culture. Mashup artists who layer data, music, or video together are the new hip-hop artists. Mashups that borrow footage from a solitary movie, such as *Back to the Future,* can easily create an entirely new story line for it. One popular mashup theme is taking the gay-cowboy theme of *Brokeback Mountain* and applying it to other movies, for example, *Back to the Future.* Scenes from the 1985 Michael J. Fox and Christopher Lloyd film are set to *Brokeback*'s mournful theme, by Gustavo Santaolalla, creating a new and, well, dramatic two-minute story line of forbidden love. It's *Brokeback to the Future.* Is it worth watching? As with any entertainment, quality is a matter of taste. Scenes and dialogue taken out of their original context and set to an emotionally driven musical score can be startling. And pretty entertaining. A popular mashup on YouTube that's been viewed more than 200,000 times is a 1:20 faux movie trailer that borrows scenes from the film *The Shining.* In its original form, Stanley Kubrick's evocative film chronicles a writer's descent into madness and murder. In the hands of a mashup artist, *The Shining* becomes *Shining,* a family comedy with a happy ending, replete with contemporary, soaring music and a new voice-over. The transformation is remarkable and, for those who have seen the original movie, laugh-out-loud funny. Some mashup artists choose to remain anonymous, while others post a handle at the end of the video to demonstrate their prowess or availability as an editor. Although copyright owners fret about derivative works and the absence of licensing fees, the mashup artists carry on, providing plenty of free, newfound exposure in a two- or three-minute commercial for movies that may have been forgotten by older audiences or never seen by younger ones.

With social media still in its infancy, understanding its potential will take years. Traditional publishers and broadcasters have had decades to perfect their craft and standards. When amateurs create their own videos, blogs, or podcasts, the reaction among some culture critics is to complain it's all a bunch of junk—what value is there to a video of kids lip-synching in front of their webcams?

Who cares about some cat-themed blog? The arguments against amateur culture go further—Wikipedia is untrustworthy, You-Tube is a waste of time, and MySpace is dangerous. The writer Douglas Adams described a similar reaction in 1999 among people who thought the same about the Internet:

> Imagine trying to apply any of those criticisms to what you hear on the telephone. Of course you can't "trust" what people tell you on the web anymore than you can "trust" what people tell you on megaphones, postcards, or in restaurants. Working out the social politics of who you can trust and why is, quite literally, what a very large part of our brain has evolved to do. For some batty reason we turn off this natural skepticism when we see things in any medium which require a lot of work or resources to work in, or in which we can't easily answer back—like newspapers, television, or granite. Hence "carved in stone."

Although it's still a developing idea, Web 2.0 is not a fluke. To build an argument as to why, we turn to Thomas Kuhn. He spent his career studying the history of science and philosophizing about its impact on culture. His most famous thesis was that the history of science has been marked by a "series of peaceful interludes punctuated by intellectually violent revolutions." In those revolutions "one conceptual world view is replaced by another." Kuhn called the traditionally held view of the world a paradigm. But if enough substantive, wholesale changes occurred within that view, whether it's in the way we buy or sell products, learn or accumulate knowledge, or interact with our communities, then we graduate to a new worldview. Kuhn called that a paradigm shift. Web 2.0 could be considered a paradigm shift because so many wholesale changes are taking place in the world of technology.

Like biology, technology is part of an evolutionary ecosystem. In the first five to six years of the 21st century, key technologies that facilitate the rise of citizen-created content and citizen marketers have been getting faster and more powerful. Inventor and futurist Ray Kurzweil argues that the early years of the 21st century are in the midst of a paradigm shift. In his fascinating book *The Singularity Is Near,* Kurzweil compiles a wealth of data and math to argue that the speed, capacity, bandwidth, and overall power of computers and electronic gadgets has begun to *double* every year. Furthermore, Kurzweil contends the overall rate of adopting new paradigms, or the rate at which society and culture make wholesale changes to their ways of doing things, is currently doubling every decade. "That is, the time to adopt new paradigms is going down by half each decade," he states. "At this rate, technological progress in the 21st century will be equivalent to 200 centuries of progress." Our tools are getting bionic.

If Kurzweil's calculations are correct and maintain their trajectory, they seem destined to retire Moore's Law. Intel cofounder Gordon Moore theorized that the number of transistors that could fit on a chip would double roughly every 18 months. Moore's Law turned out to be the principal barometer of technological growth and innovation until, at least, the turn of the century. Moore's Law has been applied primarily to the electronics and semiconductor industries, but it has influenced the development of computer hard drives, cell phones, computer games— just about anything that relies on a computer chip. Moore's Law either reliably predicted the available power of computer circuits, or manufacturers adhered to Moore's Law as a production goal and kept it a self-fulfilling prophecy. The power behind technological tools is no longer at a gradual incline; it's tipped upward and gone exponential, when numbers in the chart are multiplied, not just added. Exponential growth in computer storage capacity allowed Google to leapfrog Yahoo and Hotmail and offer one gigabyte of Web e-mail storage for free when the portals offered just one-quarter of that. (They quickly matched Google's offer.) Kurzweil says this growing power is contributing to a paradigm shift, giving scientists the ability to make stuff exponentially more powerful because existing stuff is already significantly powerful. What this means for nonscientists is that the customized, million-dollar tools Steven Spielberg used to create and edit the scarily life-like dinosaurs in his 1993 film *Jurassic Park* are now essentially available for anyone at Amazon and Best Buy to install on their Mac or PC.

For someone hoping to create sophisticated content that appeals to friends, communities, or the world, suddenly the future is looking a lot less expensive.

In what could be considered evidence supporting Kurzweil's contention of a broad paradigm shift, the rise of the citizen marketer is being fueled by two distinct technological realities: speedy broadband connections and affordable digital tools.

Broadband subscriptions have reached a saturation point, making the Internet significantly more accessible and enhancing its network effect of when something becomes more valuable based on the number of people using it. Millions of everyday people now have the bandwidth to publish and broadcast more sophisticated content while offering their audiences a voice, a vocation, and a vote. Broadband is the linchpin for online content creation; home broadband users account for two-thirds of all content created online, according to an authoritative study compiled by Pew Internet & American Life Project, a nonprofit organization that dedicates itself to studying American trends. In the

21st century, broadband usage reached a significant point: by March 2006, 84 million American adults had broadband at home. That was a 40 percent jump over the same period a year earlier. Why? A significant number of Americans dropped their pokey dial-up connections and opted for higher-speed connections, largely thanks to falling prices spurred on by price wars between phone companies and cable companies. Outside the United States, broadband adoption rates grew quickly, too. At the end of 2005, nearly 139 million people in the world subscribed to DSL. Yearly worldwide growth was 42 percent, meaning 800,000 people were subscribing to DSL every week. An industry adding nearly a million new customers per week is growing exponentially. The European Union was the biggest adopter of DSL in 2005: 16.7 million people signed up for DSL. The EU alone accounts for almost 35 percent of the world market. But for individual countries, China is the most connected: 26 million people were power surfing at home by the end of 2005. Curiously, the United States lags in all of this growth. At the end of 2005, the country was still 12th overall for broadband subscribers per 100 inhabitants. (The top five countries were Iceland, Korea, Netherlands, Denmark, and Switzerland.)

What do all of these figures mean? More broadband users mean more citizen content creators. It means more people who have the tools and access to rant and rave on blogs, podcasts, and social media sites about products, services, and brands. It means more Filters, Fanatics, Facilitators, and Firecrackers. Companies with global brands face new challenges as their call centers are democratized, presenting them with altogether new cultural and linguistic challenges. Companies that once neatly controlled lines of global demarcation will find customers don't care about corporate organization charts and business units. A brand is a brand, no matter where it's based or who manages its countries or regions.

For departments that develop products or create marketing and public relations plans, the democratization of personal expression presents altogether new (and, we hope, interesting) challenges for working with customers and noncustomers alike. People are buying products and services in one country and blogging about them in another. Small but determined groups of citizen marketers will fill the natural voids of the support centers for many well-known and well-loved products. How companies tacitly accept or officially acknowledge peer-based support will affect word of mouth. As we have already seen, the 4 *F*s have the tools and the means to publish and broadcast their stories of product experiences.

After speedy broadband connections, the second distinct technological reality is more affordable tools. The prices for software, audio equipment, and digital or video cameras have dropped dramatically, enabling millions of people to become more proficient online-content creators, publishers, and broadcasters. Citizen content creators rely on four primary tools to create that content: digital still and video cameras, cell phones, and computers.

Digital still and video cameras are the big-cat catalyzers of social media. The number of monthly visitors for two of the big social media sites—MySpace and Flickr—are in the tens of millions. One reason why they are so popular: they have made their sites photo-friendly, especially for cell-phones equipped with cameras. Digital cameras are becoming more powerful and less expensive at an exponential rate. In 2000, the average retail price of a digital camera was $499. By 2005, the average price had dropped by almost half, to $265, even as camera resolutions improved and features were added. The accessories that extend the functionality of digital cameras have fallen in price even more dramatically. A one-gigabyte flash memory card is a must-have for serious photographers. It can store about 3,700 photos of very good quality (two megapixels for each image) or about 409 images of excellent quality (five megapixels for each image). In 2003 Office Depot sold one-gigabyte flashcards for $429. Two years later, the same flashcards sold for $99.

As a combined market, digital cameras and video cameras are rich with sales. In 2000, the industry research firm Mintel said $3.6 billion of still and digital cameras were sold in the United States. By 2005, accounting for inflation, sales had basically doubled, to $6.7 billion. Cameras that take still photos are the clear sales leaders, and that's good news for sites that cater to amateur photographers. Mintel says $5.1 billion of digital cameras were sold in 2005, versus $1.6 billion for video cameras. The challenge for the 173 video sites that competed with one another in 2005, including 85 that hosted and shared videos, is a bit different. Many of them compete for the attention of webcam users. Webcams, the tiny, eyeball-looking devices encased in plastic, are fairly affordable for the average broadband user—usually about $100—and they plug directly into a computer. Two companies—Logitech and Creative Technologies—own about three-quarters of the webcam market. Creative is based in Singapore, and numbers for its business are difficult to discern, but Logitech's business reflects the spirited growth of amateur video creators. Sales of Logitech webcams grew from $166 million in 2004 to $273 million in 2006, an increase of 64 percent. In the years ahead, as video-sharing sites teach the amateur culture how to create inspiring or engaging content, the future of the webcam business looks promising.

The majority of the content creators online tend to be young, and they're getting younger. One research group reported in 2006 that "children are actively using personal music devices, digital cameras, and DVD players by age 7—some six months earlier than a year ago. Twice as many kids aged 4 to 14 owned personal

music devices and digital cameras in 2005, while cell-phone ownership in the age group has shot up 50 percent since (2005)." If
you think teenagers are already causing disruption with their cell
phones and digital cameras, just wait until ten-year-olds create
their own content and form their own networks. For executives
who grew up using electric typewriters to write their school
reports, the world has changed dramatically, and the world of
instant content creation may seem mystifying. But those who
have grown up using digital tools cannot imagine a world of Wite-
Out, carbon paper, Sony Walkmans, or even VCRs. Digital content atomizes time, compressing reality and the perception of
media in ways that may never be fathomable to someone who
didn't grow up enmeshed in that experience.

It took 50 years for POTS, or plain old telephone service, to
reach a significant level of usage in the United States, but it took
10 years for cell phones to reach the same level. That's how indis-
pensable cell phones have become to modern life. In a five-year
period alone, from 1999 to 2004, cell-phone sales and subscriptions increased 144 percent, making it a $112 billion industry.
For citizen marketers, a "smartphone" is standard equipment.
That's a phone that can send and receive e-mail, surf the Web,
take pictures, play music and videos, and even make phone calls.
It is the original Star Trek Communicator come to life.

To send all of this data to and fro, the cell-phone companies
invested billions of dollars into what they called 3G, or third-
generation, high-speed wireless networks. At the end of 2005, at
least 156 million Americans signed up for 3G networks. Citizen
marketers figure into this picture because Pew says 41 percent of
cell-phone owners use them as content tools. They check news,
weather, and who has commented on their blog. They write blog
posts, upload pictures from events, and participate in voting systems. Eight percent of American cell-phone owners say they have

used their phones to vote in television contests like *American Idol* (and pay for the privilege, no less). Eight percent is 24 million Americans. That's the equivalent of every single person in New York City, Chicago, London, and Sydney demonstrating their willingness to vote on behalf of a commercial enterprise, even if they have to pay a poll tax. More than half of American kids aged 12 to 14 own a mobile phone, and almost 80 percent of Europeans own a mobile phone. As we shape our tools, our tools shape us.

The popularity of mobile phones has sparked the creation of dozens of cell-phone-specific citizen-marketer Web sites. The Treo cell phone, made by Palm, enjoys a devoted following. At least six separate amateur Web sites are devoted to it. Most of the amateur sites dissect, discuss, and review Treo rumors and facts, problems and solutions, and new hardware and software accessories. They are de facto customer support sites, minus the warranty guarantee. When the Treo was first unveiled in 2003, I (Jackie) learned firsthand about the tremendous value of the citizen-marketer sites. While waiting for Verizon Wireless to make the Treo compatible with its network in 2004, I put myself onto a waiting list and waited eight months to be among the first who could use the smartphone on Verizon's network. When the phone finally arrived and I set up my e-mail account on it, incoming mail worked fine but outgoing mail did not. I called Verizon's customer support center, but that turned out to be a waste of an hour. It was a frustrating moment.

On a whim, I typed "Treo 600 e-mail problems" into Google. The first page of results highlighted a thread at *TreoCentral.com* that described my issue exactly. I found post after post on the site from people who described my problem along with their suggested solutions. The consensus solution: install third-party e-mail software. Dozens of posts evangelized an e-mail program called SnapperMail from Snapperfish. A few clicks later, I purchased and downloaded the program and installed it on my phone. A few clicks later, presto—incoming *and* outgoing mail. Treo's customers had shared their collective knowledge about the product and its limitations at an independent, democratized Web site that was essentially a real-time knowledge-management center. Its interface to the outside world was Google. The TreoCentral community knew more about the product, its limitations, and solutions to overcome those limitations than Verizon. In this case, the congregation was smarter than the preacher.

The PC is about to reach beyond the borders of the industrialized world. Nicholas Negroponte, the founder of MIT's Media Lab, launched the One Laptop Per Child project in 2005 to put a wireless, hand-cranked laptop into the hands of children in developing nations such as Brazil, China, Egypt, Nigeria, and Thailand for about $135 to $140 per machine. By using stripped-down versions of open-source software and taking advantage of rapidly falling component prices, Negroponte is trying to ride the wave of technological democratization by gentrifying the elitism of computer ownership. Culture could be globally democratized. The OLPC project hopes to begin making what's called "sub-$100 PCs" available to parts of the world beginning in 2007. The democratization of technology is beginning to take root in parts of the world where poverty is the norm and technology is poorer. If Negroponte's plan works, a kid growing up in an impoverished section of Cairo will have access to a new world, literally and figuratively, filled with free tools that enable him to become a publisher just as easily as a kid in front of a computer screen in London or Berlin. With a sub-$100 PC, that kid could write a blog, listen to or create a podcast, subscribe to RSS feeds, create a MySpace page, and watch videos on YouTube.

The other trends fueling the rise of citizen content creators are demographic and social. Forrester Research says that greater numbers of people are looking to technology for "social purposes." Especially youngsters. Twelve- to 17-year-olds in the United States spend 17 percent more time online than adults for personal reasons and 155 percent more time instant messaging. That daughter or niece of yours who has six instant-message screens open while talking on her cell phone in one ear with an iPod bud in the other and a YouTube video playing in the background on her laptop is multitasking her way into the future of media.

The societal research by Pew, Forrester, and Nielsen BuzzMetrics indicates that it is the young gadget-hounds who seem to have the most influence on the opinions of people in their existing online and off-line networks. They are mastering powerful new tools that enable them to become publishers and broadcasters in ways that existing traditional media outlets either admire with awe or fear with loathing.

CHAPTER FOUR

Everyone Is a Publisher; Everyone Is a Broadcaster

We become what we behold.
We shape our tools and then our tools shape us.

Marshall McLuhan, *Understanding Media: The Extensions of Man*

Could it be that the Romans 2,100 years ago were the first bloggers?

Around 130 B.C., a group of intrepid citizens began to write and publish Rome's daily news. They painstakingly carved short stories into pieces of stone and metal and hung them in public places, such as the Forum, the central square of Roman daily life. The Roman writers called their postings *Acta Diurna,* loosely translated as "daily acts." For 300 years, they reported on senate votes, legal notices, trial outcomes, and results of the gladiator fights. (Perhaps we have the Romans to thank for today's box scores.) More commonly, the *Acta Diurna* described various miracles, funerals, sacrifices, and the amorous adventures of well-known Roman citizens.

It's oddly reassuring to think that gossipy accounts of the love lives of well-known citizens make the *Acta Diurna* not unlike today's gossipy "Page Six" of the *New York Post*. It seems we humans demonstrate an inherent desire for news that could affect our lives, tempered with a dollop of celebrity news. Since none of the *Acta Diurna* have survived intact, scholars are unclear if they were written under the authority of the Roman government or represent the earliest form of the today's press. They do agree that carving a story onto a piece of stone or wood wasn't efficient. It took nearly 1,500 years, but a tool created by a young German would dramatically change the way culture and collective intelligence are shaped.

Johann Gutenberg had the entrepreneurial spirit to solve big problems. His German hamlet was home to 350 monasteries and convents, and they had an unyielding demand for printed religious materials. Gutenberg was living in a time of history when most Europeans had little, if any, concept of scientific or historical truth. Education was largely administered by the church in Rome, which was the western bookend of Europe to Constantinople's bookend on the east near Asia. In the early 1400s, when Gutenberg was a young man, he witnessed the ceaseless bickering between the two city-states over one another's authority and the control of religious doctrine. Their disputes had led to the election of three simultaneous popes, which was called the Great Schism. It was a time of tremendous cultural uncertainty and unrest. Among the many reasons for the schism was the lack of consistency in Bibles, prayer books, and hymnals. Nearly every printed material was written by hand. That made it easy for genuine errors and deliberate ones to appear and propagate. As the historian John Man wrote in his biography of Gutenberg, "A scribe would be hard-pressed to copy more than two high-quality, densely packed pages a week—one 1,272-page commentary on the Bible took two scribes five years to complete." Imagine waiting five years for a scribe to copy J. K. Rowling's latest *Harry Potter* installment.

Gutenberg's genius was recognizing the need to make a perfect copy of a publication in days, not years. Through much trial and error, he perfected the production of perfect replicas of the letters of the alphabet by pouring molten silver ore into a mold. Once cooled, the letters could be arranged into words and lines of type. The type was movable from line to line, not permanently carved into or embossed onto a single die like a piece of wood or metal. The printing press was born, and it was about to dramatically change western Europe.

The scholar Elizabeth L. Eisenstein said the printing press eventually "ripped apart the social and structural fabric of life in Western Europe and reconnected it in new ways that gave shape to modern social patterns. The availability of printed materials made possible societal, cultural, familial, and industrial changes facilitating the Renaissance, the Reformation, and the scientific revolution." The first rulers to be disrupted were the religious ones. Christianity had controlled Europe for 1,000 years prior to the printing press, but now religious leaders could create and share their own interpretations of religion. Martin Luther's Protestant Reformation was a "movement that was shaped at the very outset (and in large part ushered in) by the new powers of the press," Eisenstein declared in her authoritative book *The Printing Press as an Agent of Change.* In just three years, between 1517 and 1520, Luther's 30 publications probably sold more than 300,000 copies. That's a significant number of books, even by modern standards. Collected knowledge could be spread more effectively, in greater volume and detail. Mass-produced books about history, laws, and science made it possible for city-states and nations to share their knowledge, teachings, and beliefs with greater numbers of people. Truth was no longer the purview of a dominant entity. Knowledge was replicable.

In the decades after Gutenberg first put paper against lines of movable type, the printing press made the production of books—in fact, the production of knowledge—a catalyst for changing the culture. A new cultural die had been cast. Truth had been democratized. Society had been wrecked and rebuilt in new and egalitarian ways.

~

As Gutenberg's printing press revolutionized the world of the 15th century and thereafter, so too did radio and television dramatically alter the landscape of 20th-century culture. Marshall McLuhan was an early observer of television's power to reshape culture. In the early 1960s, he wrote: "A new form of politics is emerging, and in ways we haven't yet noticed. The living room has become a voting booth. Participation via television in freedom marches, in war, revolution, pollution, and other events is changing everything."

McLuhan argued that electronic media were making the world smaller as borders became irrelevant. Because of electronic media, the world would eventually coalesce into tribal forms of a "global village," an idea (and phrase) that lives on today. As television started to exert its influence, it created an unavoidable friction: "Our official culture is striving to force the new media to do the work of the old," he wrote. "These are difficult times because we are witnessing a clash of cataclysmic proportions between two great technologies." It was a clash between print and television. Arguably, television won. The Vietnam War and the Civil Rights movement dominated American politics because of television. Because of television, the Vietnam War shaped Americans' perception of war and politics for a generation. Since then, national political campaigns are managed largely for the benefit of television audiences. For decades, television has been the dominant force in shaping our culture of ideas and reality itself. If anything, print serves as the reality check or antidote to the inauthentic reality that television so often creates.

Clashes between traditional media and the emerging ones are inevitable, whether it's between 15th century medieval artists and the printing press or personal computers and cell phones versus the living room as the voting booth. Today, social media are forcing traditional media to reconsider their dominant, one-way publishing and broadcasting models as they struggle to bridge the gap between control and participation. McLuhan may have imagined something like the Internet, but it would take 40 years before technology would catch up to his imagination. When it did, one powerful catalyst fueling the emerging online citizen culture is the blog.

In the beginning, blogs were online journals—the equivalent of a diary entry written in the privacy of the bedroom, then locked and hid underneath the bed. Blogs appeared almost as quickly as the Web did in the 1990s. Justin Hall was one of the Web's earliest diarists. As a student at Swarthmore College, he wrote lengthy observations about jobs, relationships, family, and his life's most intimate details. His open-book journal and life accounted for 4,800 posts in total. The *New York Times* proclaimed him the "very first blogger," and his work helped established the early practice of blog-as-confessional and pulpit. He did this reliably for 11 years, and then abruptly stopped in early 2005 for a few months before resuming.

"The main takeaway from my life led in public, online? Correspondence with other searchers," Hall said in 2005. "People who found me because they were looking for meaning or self or whatever I was looking for. I value that lack of isolation I felt as I poured myself into my web pages."

Young Justin helped lead the way for the individual as publisher. He shared his private thoughts in a most public manner by creating his own Web pages, and it paved the way for the creation of Web-based publishing tools like LiveJournal in 1999. After seven years, LiveJournal was hosting ten million accounts. (The service offers a mix of free and paid tools. Also launching at nearly the same time was a similar company called Blogger, which was eventually purchased by Google.) The rise of online journalizing began with teenagers, as many trends do. Of the LiveJournal account holders who had volunteered their birth date, the vast majority were between the ages of 15 and 23. Two-thirds were female. Nearly all were American.

Mena Trott started a personal online journal in early 2001 and called it Dollarshort. She was a 24-year-old designer living in California. As her journal grew in popularity, Trott was increasingly unhappy with the software that powered it. Then the small design studio she worked at with her husband, Ben, abruptly closed in September 2001. That got her thinking. "Faced with the prospect of looking for new jobs, Ben and I decided to take some time off and develop our own weblogging tool that we would share with some of our friends," Trott writes, appropriately enough, on her blog. A month later, they released the blogging software they had written. The whole time they'd called it Serge. Just before launch, Trott thought of Gutenberg and the impact he'd had on publishing. They called it Movable Type.

"The morning of the Movable Type 1.0 release, Ben and I sat anxiously in front of our computers, fingers ready to make Movable Type available to the public. Within the first hour over 100 people had downloaded the software." Instead of charging directly for the software, the Trotts asked for donations. Two years later they launched a hosted version of the software called Typepad for people who wanted to blog immediately, within minutes, without having to download and install software. Five years later, their company, Six Apart, owned the blogging market with its range of tools. The company that Mena and Ben Trott started in their San

Francisco apartment was on its way to helping millions of people become publishers and build worldwide audiences, and it would eventually cause traditional media companies to reconsider their ways of interacting with readers.

That the Trotts called their software Movable Type was a prescient decision. Millions of blogs have since been created, and they're on the radars of big companies, if not drawn up in their playbooks; senior executives from General Motors, Southwest Airlines, Sun, HP, and *Amazon.com* blog regularly and engage in back-and-forth discussions with everyday people. Although formal research has yet to correlate the regular readers of company blogs with more spending or higher referral rates, we can assume that readers' investment of time and attention with company blogs indicates loyalty.

For companies, starting and maintaining a blog is creating a real-time customer-feedback system. Blog readers talk with one another, spur ideas, identify problems, or debate semantics. It's not a quantifiable feedback system, but it does create a front-row seat for companies interested in the real-time opinions of people who are well-educated, better paid, and leading indicators of trends. Just as Gutenberg's printing press did 600 years ago, blogs are democratizing the control of information and knowledge by diffusing it to a wider swath of people. Knowledge is being replicated at rates beyond the scope and capability of print. If every blogger is a publisher, then every blog is also a platform—a stage in the middle of the virtual piazza. The challenge is to get the people to pay attention.

Six Apart was a blogging pioneer, but it's a challenge to quantify the company's reach. As a privately held company, it declines to share data on Movable Type installations or the number of bloggers it hosts on Typepad. On the other hand, Microsoft provides a glimpse of data about its operation. A year and a half after it launched, Windows Live Spaces, a free blogging service, was attracting 100 million unique visitors per month. Nearly one in seven Internet users in the world was visiting a Spaces blog. One reason may be that Spaces appears to have attracted a significant number of Chinese bloggers. In a paper titled "24 Hours in the Blogosphere," researcher Matthew Hurst analyzed all of the "pings" captured by servers that blog-hosting services automatically send out when someone has updated his or her blog. In his 24-hour sample, Hurst found that bloggers in China were by far Spaces' most active bloggers, outnumbering American bloggers by a factor of four. Its third most active blogging country was Taiwan, closely behind the United States. Japan and Brazil, respectively, rounded out the top five. From this sample at least, we can presume the dominant language among blogs on Spaces is Chinese. With a population of more than 1.3 billion, China may theoretically become the blogging capital of the world, but freedom of speech in China is an ongoing experiment.

Just as it had accomplished with Windows, Microsoft's trajectory was to capture a sizable, if not majority share, of personal blogs. On the Internet, the same as in television and radio, the company that attracts the most visitors allows it to command the highest prices for the "virtual billboards." It could be argued that blogs are no different than personal homepages of the 1990s, but the arrival and growth of LiveJournal, Movable Type, and Spaces demonstrate considerable demand among everyday people for easy-to-use tools to become publishers. Homepages of the 1990s required basic knowledge of HTML. Modern blogging tools do not. Hence, their spiraling demand.

In any new market, money follows demand. When Rupert Murdoch's News Corporation purchased teen-driven social-networking site MySpace for $580 million, the business world took MySpace a lot more seriously. A few months later, AOL bought Weblogs Inc., a network of blogs focused on topics from scuba diving to gadgets, for a reported $25 million. Measuring money flow is interesting, but it does not yet measure the influence of social media on popular culture, and vice versa. For that, we turn to a company called Technorati.

Technorati functions a bit like NASDAQ: it actively promotes the blog industry, tracks its growth, and ranks the relative value of the millions of blogs competing for attention. Attention is typically measured via the "trackback"—the action when one blogger links to another. Technorati attempts to follow the blogging world's trackbacks. It tends to assign more weight of influence to blogs with more trackbacks than ones with fewer. Like power-law distributions that we discussed in Chapter 2, a disproportionately small number of blogs attract the most traffic compared to the total number of blogs in existence. To get noticed among the tens of millions of blogs usually requires one to be a prolific linker. (To be fair, not all blogs clamor for attention—some are kept primarily as an event or life diary or a diary of a person's kids or dogs.) Technorati is also a search engine, and its results often indicate the most popular topics being discussed online at any particular moment. For instance, if you want a snapshot of what people are saying about Hilton Hotels, Technorati will search its index and return the citations it finds on blogs. As a word-of-mouth indicator, Technorati is sometimes a red-alert alarm. Its front page displays a list of the hour's most-used search terms; some terms arrive several days later as stories in traditional media.

When Technorati first began tracking blogs in March 2003, there were perhaps a few thousand of them. Since then, Technorati has found that the total number of blogs roughly doubles every six months. (In September 2006, Technorati reported it was tracking 55 million blogs.) It has been a sort of Moore's Law whose lifespan remains uncertain. When the data of the number of blogs are drawn on a chart, the first 1.5 years of data resemble the gentle incline a roller coaster follows out of the station. Beginning around January 2005, the data and the roller-coaster car turn dramatically upward, the ascent powered by the simple arithmetic of doubling numbers. In three years, the blogosphere had increased a hundredfold.

One natural question about that growth is, when does it stop, or at least flatten? "There are only so many human beings in the world!" Technorati's founder wrote on his blog, detailing yet another crazy growth curve. "It has to slow down." Perhaps not just yet. Data aggregated by Miniwatts Marketing Group found more than 1 billion people were online in 2006. Asia led the way, with 380 million citizens online, followed by 294 million Europeans and 227 million North Americans. In all, about 16 percent of the world's population was surfing. If people are expressive beings and they find that a blog is a fundamental tool for expression, the growth in blogs would seem to be very much in its early stages. That's the first reason why the growth of new blogs has yet to subside. A second reason: what happens when things other than humans start blogging? What if cars start blogging? Or jets? Or animals? Do we count the "blogjects"?

That's what University of Southern California researcher Julian Bleecker calls things that collect data, then disseminate them via social media. Case in point: flocks of homing pigeons scattered in a few cities across California began collecting data about air pollution in the summer of 2006 and posted it as text messages to the PigeonBlog. Each bird carries a tiny cell-phone transmitter and air-pollution monitor. They transmit data in real time while flying, resting, or eating. With their tool kits attached to their bodies with Velcro, the pigeons map pollution levels in real time, while their locations and routes are pinpointed to a satellite view of a Google map. Watching their flight patterns on the map is fascinating enough, but paired with pollution data, their work creates a new realm of blog mashup. The pigeons are mobile bloggers, and tiny cameras around their necks allow the project's coordinators to take aerial photos and instantly post them online. Even if birds, bears, or boars are the bloggers of the future, it'll be up to humans to wrap their data in context and meaning. An animal version of *The Truman Show* could mean one day that a Canadian grizzly is an authoritative voice on precipitation, pollution, or poaching. If the universe of objects is infinite, so, too, is their potential to blog. The potential of blogjects to raise our collective knowledge is remarkable.

It only took a few years for blogs to leave the fringes and become the masses.

~

If blogs were parents, podcasts would be their firstborn.

Podcasting makes possible what has eluded radio listeners since the dawn of broadcasting: an easy way to subscribe to a show and then pause, rewind, or fast-forward it without relying on cassette tapes. Like blog posts, podcasts are digital files delivered automatically to subscribers as feeds. The FCC is joyfully excluded from regulating its content. Even during its first few years of development—podcasts began to appear regularly in 2003—podcasting was already democratizing elements of traditional radio broadcasting. Since the dawn of radio, anyone with a microphone and a tape recorder could have been a broadcaster, but to reach tens of thousands or millions of listeners required a license from the FCC. With a computer and iTunes, anyone can be a broadcaster and reach tens of thousands of listeners without the FCC's permission. Search Apple Computer's iTunes podcast directory for "baby" and you'll discover at least 18 amateur pod-casts including *PregTASTIC Pregnancy Podcast* and *Baby Talk Radio*. Some of the more popular podcasters have audiences whose size rivals traditional radio shows. *Keith and the Girl* is a daily talk show hosted by a New York couple, Keith Malley and Chemda Khalili. Each day, they talk about the minutiae of their lives, sometimes in foul language, and they attract 50,000 listeners per episode. The FCC would not approve, and that may very well be one of the show's success factors.

Citizen marketers are among the early adopters of podcasting tools, and they are creating shows devoted to brands and products. Paul Dennis, a professor at Black Hills State University, hosts *The Real Deadwood Podcast,* a bimonthly variety show from Deadwood, South Dakota. It's for fans of the HBO television show *Deadwood,* and Dennis combines interviews, entertainment, and news from both Deadwoods. *The Meandering Mouse Podcast* is a bimonthly podcast hosted by Disney enthusiast "Jeff from Houston." He says his audio "meanderings" in Disney amusement parks emphasize "all those little details that create magical memories."

The democratization of radio now means that some radio shows are downloadable, and some broadcasters are adapting to the changing marketplace. In 2006 National Public Radio launched an ambitious effort to make more than 300 of the shows it airs on local stations available as podcasts. NPR's listeners loved the idea; after a few months time, they were downloading two million podcasts per week. With such a promising start, NPR plans to build online communities around its more popular shows and podcasts. "That's our dream," is how Eric Nuzum, NPR's director of programming and acquisitions, described it.

Other than punching preset buttons, listeners have never had much control of radio. But the radio-on-demand feature inherent in podcasting portends an uncertain future for broadcasters. In

June 2006, Nielsen Analytics found that 9 million Americans downloaded podcasts that month alone. Ten percent of the 1,700 people Nielsen surveyed were podcast superusers; they downloaded eight or more podcasts per week. What may concern some traditional radio stations was that 38 percent of the surveyed users said they listen to the radio less because of podcasts. Extrapolated across 9 million Americans, that means 3.4 million Americans listened to terrestrial radio less because of podcasts. Let's play the scenario out in the future. In a 2005 report about podcasting, Bride Ratings estimated that by 2010, about 63 million Americans will be downloading podcasts. Should 38 percent of podcast listeners continue to listen less often to the radio, that equals 23.9 million Americans. Terrestrial radio was already declining in listenership; 194 million Americans were radio listeners in 2005, down from 203 million a year earlier. The growth of podcasts means that at least 71 million Americans might listen to radio even less often than they do now.

With millions of iPods in circulation, travel is a popular podcasting topic. The online travel agency Orbitz has created a podcast series about travel destinations. Another travel business, TravelCommons, calls itself "the voice of the business traveler" and records weekly "travel stories recorded in hotel bathrooms around the world." Podcasts seem to have an especially promising future for businesses that sell to other businesses. A weekly podcast by Energy Smart News focuses on the lighting industry. Each week, its host interviews the makers of light switches and bulbs. Fitness Business Radio focuses exclusively on covering the business of the fitness industry. At MIT and other schools around the world, professors record their lectures and then make them available as podcasts. Niche markets are being served in ways meant to appeal to busy businesspeople who travel with iPods, the icon of podcasting.

Video podcasts are cousins to audio podcasts. Video podcasts are subscribable videos that can be watched on the computer or downloaded to a handheld video device, like the video iPod. They are often amateur-created, Web-based television shows with weekly or daily episodes. Video podcasts are available from iTunes or directly from their accompanying blog. One of the most well-known amateur video podcasts is Rocketboom, a daily three-minute take on Internet news and culture. Produced with a staff of four, the show had 300,000 subscribers after its first two years. That's more viewers than almost any single local newscast in America.

RSS is short for Really Simple Syndication, but it's not always simple to explain or understand.

One way to describe RSS is that it makes anything on the Web "subscribable." Blogs, podcasts, discussion forums, even parts of entire Web sites, like *Amazon.com,* are subscribable with RSS. To ensure you receive everything a well-known blogger writes, subscribe to her RSS feed. Want Microsoft's latest press releases the moment they're released? Subscribe to Microsoft's press-release feed. RSS is actually a mask atop a broader, technical definition (specifically, how content is wrapped within an XML file format), so the emerging, user-friendly term is *feed.* A feed is a free, instant-data delivery vehicle for a publisher, who can be anyone or anything. Human, machine, or as we discussed earlier, animal.

The promise of feeds is that subscribers elect to receive data. If they tire of the publisher or their data sent through the feed, subscribers simply turn if off, like a spigot. For the creators of amateur content, feeds democratize the worlds of publishing and broadcasting in at least four distinct ways:

1. Feeds do not consume energy. Newspapers and magazines operate a complex printing and delivery model to send their work to tens or hundreds of thousands of subscribers, requiring infrastructure and cash flow. Bloggers, podcasters, or feed creators simply send turn on their data feed, and subscribers tap it or turn it off. In the world of digital bits, the number of subscribers is irrelevant. It costs an RSS feed publisher no more to have an audience of hundreds of thousands than it does to have one hundred.

2. Feeds are free. Feeds do not use e-mail addresses, and that's a relief to information hounds, who must sort the spam from relevant e-mail items. Reliable e-mail management systems require an up-front or ongoing investment. There is a trade-off with this pact. Feed subscribers are anonymous because RSS does not rely on any personally identifying information. That keeps the unrelenting solicitations from Nigerian princes with stashed-away money out of the feed universe, but it also means audience members are invisible until they make themselves known in other forms, such as e-mail. That's part of the blueprints for feeds.

3. Feeds are almost instantaneous. Send your data to the feed pipe, and everyone who is prepared to receive it will do so within a few minutes. As a subscriber, how you choose to receive feeds is dependent on your comfort level with technology. It could be as simple as making them part of your Yahoo home page or designating them as a bookmarks list in your Web browser. It could be an account with a Web site designed to collect feeds. It could be a separate piece of software called an aggregator, which groups all of your feeds into a display system, much like an e-mail program does. It could be software that plugs into your

existing e-mail program. Or your cell phone. If you can imagine a future tool that is connected to the Internet, chances are it can receive a feed.

4. Feed subscribers are a tangible asset. They represent a direct line of communication, thereby giving publishers considerable power to spread data, news, gossip, or information. Feeds are one reason why word of mouth among blogs, especially among the Firecracker examples mentioned earlier, can spread quickly: feeds accelerate everything. That's the experience Dick Costolo has been having with his business, Feedburner. His company is like an air-traffic-control system that directs tens of millions of feeds from publishers to hundreds of thousands of subscribers each day. The growth in feeds parallels the growth in blogs, doubling roughly every five or six months. Like other Web 2.0 businesses, Feedburner offers most of its services for free. With venture capitalists financing his business, Costolo is staking out an early claim. As tools and systems become more sophisticated, Feedburner and other companies like it will offer premium paid services to sort or combine multiple feeds, compile data into reports, or place ads inside or along feeds.

Any device that can read formatted data has the potential to become a feed reader. That's part of the inherent power of RSS but also the cause for some of the confusion caused by its flexibility. RSS is not a product. It's a delivery system that can be used by anyone. It may help traditional media realize a long-held vision of "a customized news product." Reuters, CNN, and the BBC send headlines, news summaries, stories, or some combination of the above directly to readers via a feed. Many in the news industry had hoped e-mail would fulfill the promise for customized news delivery, but spam and the nets to stop it have largely destroyed that plan; by some estimates, more than 50 percent of all e-mail sent in the latter half of 2005 was spam.

Feeds probably drive some economists nuts. It's a free technology. It isn't owned or controlled by a company that charges for its use. Its design was hashed out by a small group of volunteers, not a group of industrial manufacturers trying to control and profit from a market. The work that has gone into making feeds a nearly universal feature of Web-based data delivery systems is emblematic of an altruistic belief held by some that technology should make our lives more productive and better.

Few stories better illustrate the ripple effects of the quickening pace of the democratization of technology than the creation of TiVo. The digital video recorder that captures television signals as you watch them, or easily records seasons of shows or programs based on keywords, is an innovation of culture-changing proportion. It rose from the smoldering ruins of another expensive Time Warner effort—the Full Service Network (FSN)—which attempted to create the first working version of viewer-controlled television.

The lead software developer for FSN was Jim Barton. Time Warner hired his employer at the time to help build FSN. But the World Wide Web arrived about a year later, and Time Warner pulled the plug soon thereafter. The promise of viewer-controlled television inspired Barton and a colleague, Mike Ramsay, to pursue the idea. One of FSN's biggest challenges was a computer operating system inside each set-top box powerful enough to make viewer-controlled television possible. The operating system they created for FSN was unsuited to its task, but Barton and Ramsay now had Linux available to them. The blueprints for this computer operating system are available for anyone to read, test, or modify. No one "owns" Linux, which means no restrictive licensing or royalty agreements exist. With Linux and cheaper hard drives and computer components (it was rumored that each set-top box in the FSN trial cost $3,000), Barton and Ramsay built their television-controlling product, TiVo, at a retail-realistic price point, shipping the first TiVos to retailers in March 1999. Television watching had been democratized. Viewers were freed from the clumsiness of VCRs and the uncompromising schedules of broadcasters. Freedom is a powerful driver, and TiVo knew it. The company boasted that 96 percent of its subscribers would never give up their TiVo service.

As with any paradigm-changing technology, the rate at which the masses buy it can be painfully slow. It took six years for TiVo to show a profit on its balance sheet. But thanks to a fiercely loyal and vocal group of customers, the word *TiVo* joined the American pop-culture vernacular. It could be argued that one reason why the company survived years of slow and unprofitable growth is *TiVoCommunity.com*. It's a free, open, and decentralized forum of support for the digital video recorder. Its 130,000 members are an uncompensated technical support team for 45,000 visitors every day. David Bott is its founder and virtual mayor.

Bott is an experienced hand at communities and forums. Before starting TiVoCommunity, he launched an online community for people who live and breathe home-theater technology. Plus, he'd once worked for the city of Gates, New York, as its director of network operations and oversaw its municipal Web sites. He has a city manager's no-nonsense mind-set. He quit his job with the city when his home-theater forum started earning him more money than the city job.

When discussions about TiVo in the home-theater forum started to heat up in late 2000, Bott recognized the potential for a stand-alone forum dedicated to TiVo. He composed a quick e-mail to TiVo, asking for its blessing. One arrived a week later. Almost immediately, TiVoCommunity assumed and has maintained a House of Commons–like mentality. Raucous debates about the company's business model, its strategic directions, its marketing, and the product's features are common. The community has also assumed some of the work of a public relations firm: it has cataloged thousands of TiVo mentions in traditional and online media. Probably more than anything, Bott says, a small but core group of TiVoCommunity members answers product-support questions. They troubleshoot issues. They spot bugs. They help customers with cable-company problems. They serve, Bott says, most often as a support person before a sale is made.

"Some people think we're TiVo," he says, emphasizing that the community is not. "But TiVo loved it. They started to grow a niche market through other people on our site. My whole philosophy in this is education and helping people make the most of what they own. TiVo was a hot product when it first came out, but it needed development and feedback to grow." Bott credits TiVo for monitoring forum discussions; by his count, 44 TiVo employees have registered with the community since its inception.

Since then, TiVoCommunity occasionally demonstrates the creative and action-oriented leaps TiVo customers will take as citizen marketers to assume ownership of a company, brand, and product. Several members created training guides on how to recognize and approach an electronics store salesperson who doesn't adequately explain TiVo's value proposition to prospective customers. TiVoCommunity has built an elaborate "help center" with several thousand threads that cover almost every imaginable problem TiVo customers encounter, from faulty remotes to problems with the company's numerous rebate offers. Several hundred threads wind their way through the "Suggestion Avenue" forum, where thousands of people have offered ideas to improve the product. Some companies may spend tens of thousands of dollars to gather what essentially amounts to the same type of data.

Bott worries about some of his TivoCommunity citizens. "Some people literally spend eight hours a day on the site," he said. "They develop personal relationships with the people and the community. It's kinda scary. Some people have asked me to close their accounts and ban their IPs because it was beginning to affect their work or family lives." Like the 1 Percenters, the TiVoCommunity members are protective of their community. They organize their own off-site conventions. They raise money for longtime members who face unexpected tragedies or disasters. They stick together because of the product. Sometimes, in spite of it.

~

MySpace and YouTube command most of the attention about social media, social networks, and why online communities form. But why are they popular?

The simple answer is they have democratized the tools of self-expression. A MySpace user has the flexibility and permission to fill her personal profile page with as many gadgets, sound files, blinking items, and eye-jarring backgrounds as she wishes. Her space, perhaps like her bedroom, can be as awesome or as ugly as she desires. She can pack it to the ceiling with digital gadgets. That makes her space stand out from the clean yet homogenous design of most corporate Web sites. Design experts who insist on uniformity of color and style for something called "brand identity" would not do well in MySpace. Teenagers are free to express their identity, form social networks, and hang out with friends. For them, MySpace is the new mall. Musicians were some of the earliest members of MySpace. The site attracted music fans on the prowl for cool, undiscovered bands. MySpace is home to more than 666,000 artists and bands. The freedom conferred to every MySpace user—including the freedom to upload music and photos and show off as a party-happy, even drunken fool—is precisely why some people love MySpace and others loathe or fear it. For the most part, it is free from overbearing adult supervision.

MySpace consistently listened to its most devoted members and provided the functionality they requested. Rather than give its users an elaborate tool set that would take months of development, the company's programmers launched a new tool every few weeks. There was always something new to try, therefore something new to play with and talk about. it was gadgets for the gadget oriented. Rupert Murdoch's purchase of MySpace probably came just in time as well. It has sunk $20 million into staff and infrastructure, including upgrading old servers and software code, problems that had hobbled the one-time king of social networks, Friendster. In July 2006, one research firm said MySpace had reached a new plateau: it was the most-visited U.S. Web site and accounted for 4.5 percent of all U.S. Internet visits. By then, MySpace was approaching 100 million member profiles. Google caught MySpace fever and signed a deal in the summer of 2006 to pay MySpace $900 million to put Google's search and advertising services on the site. With that deal alone, Rupert Murdoch had already earned his money back twice for a property he had purchased a year earlier. All of that freedom of expression combined with plenty of user-controlled tools made all the difference.

When YouTube came out of nowhere in November 2005, launched by two twentysomething entrepreneurs above a pizza parlor in San Mateo, California, it became the predominant online video-sharing site in about six months. By its six-month anniversary, YouTube was reportedly reaching more people than the Web sites of all the major television networks *and* popular yet traditional media like the *New York Times.* It was serving 100 million videos each day to 6 million people. Visitors were uploading more than 65,000 videos daily. It handily brushed off a challenge from Google, even with its army of PhDs and $4 billion in annual revenue. But why? What gave this Silicon Valley startup the momentum to stare down the most-feared online company in the world and win? How did it become the 39th most popular Web site and a sought-after partner for television networks?

Applying McLuhanesque philosophy to the question, we say that the computer has become a voting booth, and democratized communities can create the politics of influence. YouTube reflects the leading edge of social networks. Its tools are the ones to match or beat in the art and science of personal expression. The six lessons of YouTube are instructive for any organization considering creating its own democratized community.

1. YouTube was designed and built with community as its founding principle. Features like visitor-created tags, voting, and comments are the social media tools that democratize involvement. Its other functions, like creating lists of friends, favorite videos, and interest groups, allowed natural tribes to flourish. YouTube's private e-mail system encouraged registration and allowed members to contact one another without having to provide their everyday e-mail address. That provided YouTubers some measure of anonymity and helped prevent their everyday e-mail addresses from being inundated with spam. By contrast, Google Video's launch reflected a video directory service more than a social networking site. It wasn't until later that it added tools like ratings, tags, and comments.

2. YouTube made sharing content ridiculously easy. It added a "Share this video" message to the end of each video. Built-in functionality within that message made videos easy to share with friends. It smartly provided the programming code for savvy users to embed YouTube's videos directly into their personal blogs or Web sites. That gave YouTube credibility with early users and signaled it wasn't trying to control the experience or merely drive viewers back to its Web site. At Google Video, sharing videos required visitors to decipher a button called "E-mail—Blog—Post to MySpace."

3. YouTube was loaded with statistics. It displayed the number of viewings of each video, a critical data point of pride for some video creators. It displayed the number of comments for each video, the number of times other viewers voted it a "favorite," and the number of honors it won, such as "#4 Most Viewed of All Time." It displayed the number of links to each video, an evidence builder for video creators and observers who trace the routes of buzz and influence. When Google Video finally added ratings, it only displayed the overall rating of one-to-five stars. It didn't display the number of votes, viewings, or honors. Data transparency has been one of YouTube's strongest attributes. It doesn't hide data; it flaunts it. Each month throughout 2006, the traditional media trumpeted the numbers of YouTube video uploads, video viewings, and daily visitors. That serves two roles: it is evidence for professional and amateur analysts to discuss popularity, and it's a feedback tool for video creators about their creative or marketing abilities. In the YouTube universe, links are empirical evidence of popularity, evidence that can be viewed and measured by anyone in real time.

4. YouTube encouraged its users to personalize their public profile pages. Like MySpace, YouTubers can decorate their profiles like a teenager who has just discovered primary colors, even if it makes the page virtually unreadable. In YouTube parlance, anyone who uploads a video becomes a "channel," and every channel is subscribable. The most popular channels tend to be young men and women who create frequent personal video blogs, do skits, or otherwise act as entertainers. When people upload videos, they're encouraged to add "tags" (or keywords) that describe the video or its creators. YouTube visitors can also subscribe to tags. For instance, we subscribed to the tag "mcdonalds," and 11 videos were added immediately to our account. Each time we visit YouTube, our channels and tags are updated with the latest videos. Google Video did not offer a personal area for video creators, but it does offer a master Google account for individuals. As for the personalization tools, Google didn't come close to offering anything similar.

5. YouTube's user interface was restrained and simple. It embraced white space and didn't try to portray itself thematically as a place only for teens or twentysomething hipsters. That design consideration created a universally pleasing aesthetic for professionals and amateurs, young and old. YouTube's tabbed navigation atop each page wasn't revolutionary, but tabs make navigation easier. Google Video was a jumble of rows of stills and vertical lists of video titles. Its interface was blue, underlined links, fitting in with Google's overall design schema, which, besides being vaunted for simplicity, is uninspired. Google Video's cluttered design betrayed the white-space simplicity of the Google home page.

6. YouTube's search functionality, although not its strongest point, consistently bested Google Video's functionality. That's a surprising outcome from the world's search leader. YouTube let visitors sort their search returns by title, date added, view count, and rating. Google Video's visitors could only sort search returns by date and title.

In their early days of competition, Google did beat YouTube in two important areas: (1) making videos downloadable and (2) providing video content creators the means to sell their videos. For those who create multimedia presentations, a downloadable video is a big differentiator. If an Internet connection isn't available, good luck showing or sharing a YouTube video. For content creators who believe online videos are a moneymaking venture, Google Video offers a financial system for buyers and sellers. That future is uncertain; most online videos are largely viewed for free, their presentations underwritten by the growing number of advertisers.

Social networks and democratized communities are for real, and their impact in other countries is sometimes measured in double-digit figures. In South Korea, a third of the country has joined Cyworld, a Web community operated by SK Telecom. Its members create their own digital homes and fill them with an unlimited number of photos, diaries, documents, even school papers. Members decorate their spaces just as they do with their analog homes—with artwork, TV sets, and furniture. Just as they do with their real homes, Cyworldians spend real money to decorate their digital homes, enriching Cyworld as the digital landlord. When visitors stop by a digital Cyworld home, it's probably because they saw a proprietor's photo, blog posting, or furniture arrangement. Friendships on Cyworld are affirmed with the click of a button, then often blossom in the analog world. With Cyworld, perhaps more so than with most social networking communities, distinctions between the real world and the virtual world are often blurred.

There are challenges to stand-alone social networks like Cyworld, MySpace, and their dozens, if not hundreds, of competitors. The democratization of technology has leveled the playing field for entrepreneurs to create their own stand-alone networks. Increasingly, entrepreneurs in Silicon Valley launch their Web 2.0 projects financed with credit cards, not venture capitalists. The stand-alone social networks may have hundreds of competitors in the future for the Bowiechicks of the world, who focus on niche-oriented lifestyles. With their audiences largely comprised of teens and twentysomethings, it is inevitable that these social networks suffer the vagaries of catering to such a young market. A new generation of teens typically arrives armed with new expectations and a disdain for the cultural tastes of their older siblings. As homogenous communities, stand-alone social networks lack a rallying cause; their network is only as valuable as its members and their actions. The playing field has been leveled for brands, companies, and nonprofit associations, too. For a brand with a change-the-world mission, an attached social network can blossom into an integrated communication system that, like TiVoCommunity, debates strategic directions, spots bugs, catalogs media hits, offers upgrade ideas, and works to keep the brand alive. Their contributions are a deed to ownership.

In 2030, when historians and anthropologists pore through all of this data—photos, posts, tags, videos, podcasts—it will be considerably easier for them to mark the point when social media began to change the fundamental structures of the world's cultures. In the early years of the 21st century, blogs have been a significant force in democratizing the traditional notions of personal expression.

CHAPTER FIVE

Hobbies and Altruism

Say, I like the color of your car there. What's that s'posed to be?
Sort of a cross between piss yella' and puke green ain't it?

Bob Falfa, as played by Harrison Ford in *American Graffiti*

The small town of Carlisle, Pennsylvania, is known for two things: for being a central trucking hub of the American East Coast and for hosting one of the world's largest annual meetings of car enthusiasts.

Carlisle's geography naturally positions it as a hub. It's in southern Pennsylvania, tucked like sandwich meat between two hearty slices of roadway: Interstate 76 to the north and Interstate 81 to the south. The town (borough, officially) separates the two interstates and their importance as major arteries of interstate commerce. Sixty percent of the U.S. population is reachable within a day's drive of this area. A 1.2-mile stretch of Route 11 that runs through Carlisle is called the Miracle Mile. It connects the interstates and sees 5,400 trucks every day, the second-heaviest volume of truck traffic on a roadway in the country. As trucks love Carlisle, so do cars and their enthusiasts. Every year, some 500,000 of them drive their vehicles to this borough of 18,074 residents and its leafy, well-swept streets to talk about cars and sell them to one another. During "Cars at Carlisle," collectors trade specialty Corvettes, Fords, GMs, Chryslers, trucks, motorcycles, sport compacts, and vintage imports. With its small-town charm and love of cars, Carlisle is a living version of *American Graffiti.*

In keeping with Carlisle's history as a hub of collectible commerce, Eric Karkovack is right at home. For four years, in a 700-square-foot apartment on the outskirts of town, the 28-year-old Karkovack has spent part of each day building and nurturing a community of what he calls "soda activists." One thousand of them have signed up. He wrote a weekly newsletter for them. Built and maintained an elaborate Web site. Orchestrated telephone campaigns directed at bottlers. Gathered signatures for petitions. Created a hall of fame. All to convince the Coca-Cola Company and its 394 U.S. bottlers to resurrect a dead soda.

It's important to say at this point that Karkovack is genial, outgoing, and sincere. He is a Web site developer who has operated his own consulting practice since 1999. He has created Web sites for Pennsylvania radio stations, marketing agencies, and, naturally, transportation companies. He is what you might expect of a young entrepreneur: smart, confident, and calm. He's not the stereotypical image of a bullhorn-toting *activist,* a term he uses with a bit of irony. He just happens to be a very passionate fan of an alien-green, highly caffeinated soda called Surge, and it's been MIA since 2002.

The story of Surge begins in 1997, when Coca-Cola launched it with a razzle-dazzle Super Bowl commercial. It caught the attention of Karkovack, who was then 19 years old. For a while, Surge did OK as a product: 69 million cases sold in its first year. A respectable number for a niche soda. (By comparison, 1.9 billion cases of Coke Classic were sold in 1997). Two years later, Surge lost its marketing fizz. Sales dropped 25 percent, to 51.8 million cases. A year after that, Surge sales didn't, and they slid another 48 percent. Bottlers across the country reevaluated their investment in the brand. The publisher of *Beverage Digest* suspected the demise was caused by marketing inattention, saying Coke did not dedicate enough resources for it to escape the formidable shadow of Mountain Dew, which is made by Coke's archenemy, Pepsico. Like a rolling blackout, Surge disappeared from store shelves. By February 2002, most bottlers had stopped producing it.

Prior to becoming a soda activist, Karkovack was a soda hobbyist. He hung out on a Web site called BevNet. It's an online trade publication for people involved in beverage retailing. BevNet also hosts an open online forum called the BevBoard. Thousands of people fill the BevBoard with tens of thousands of posts about energy drinks, product sightings, and reviews of new products. That's where Karkovack saw a posting in April 2000 titled "SAVE SURGE!!!!!!!!!!!!!!!!!!!!!!!!!" It was the plea of Avery Lund, who saw that his favorite soda was being phased out of distribution.

The post sparked a friendship between the two young men (Lund was 16 and in high school), and they worked together on a new cause: *SaveSurge.org* launched on February 1, 2002. "The idea of getting Coke to bring back Surge was the main focus," Karkovack told us while sitting in his home office, surrounded by Surge memorabilia. "We also wanted to show that there were fans out there who cared about it. We wanted to celebrate the brand."

But why?

"One of the slogans for *SaveSurge.org* has been 'It's more than a soda; it's a way of life,'" Karkovack says. "We've got memories involved with the soda. It's not just about taste or caffeine or things like that. It's actually about a lot of great memories. A lot of my youth was spent driving around with my friends, stopping at convenience stores, always picking up a 20-ounce bottle of Surge."

As a call-to-arms Web site, *SaveSurge.org* rivals the complexity and depth of many political Web sites. It features some 500 pages of Surge testimonials, photographs of Surge marketing paraphernalia, and recipes for Surge Jell-O and Surge Cookies. Members debated activist strategies and tactics in a discussion forum. An online petition to resurrect Surge collected 13,799 signatures. Surge sightings were maintained in a searchable database; fans kept tabs on Surge found at restaurant soda fountains or convenience stores. Demand for expired Surge was economically real and profitable. Twelve-packs of the soda four years past their expiration date have sold for $152 on eBay. Not unlike what large-scale political action groups do with their members, Karkovack and Lund made it easy for fellow activists to send pre-written letters to senior Coca-Cola leaders, its consumer-affairs department, and local bottling companies. They posted phone numbers and e-mail addresses of those authorities and encouraged community members to lobby them. They made it easy for fellow SaveSurgians to create their own *SaveSurge.org* business cards and pamphlets that explained the group's mission.

"Everybody who sends something in feels like he or she is actually contributing to something . . . even if it is not as important as curing cancer or saving the environment. People want to feel a part of something," Karkovack said. That last part, the need for community, wasn't part of his original plan but has organically grown into a tangible contributor to the group's lifespan. "It really didn't start out as a community. It was more of an informational site for the first couple of months. As people started sending photos and stories in, they really built the community for us. It was just amazing to see the crazy things that people were doing for Surge and willing to fight for it." The community was the opportunity for them to fight for something, a way for the young men to test and understand the adult themes of purpose and mission.

Their mission was propelled by a smart idea: a hall of fame. Community members inducted into the SaveSurge Hall of Fame are recognized for their "time and energy as volunteers (to) fight tirelessly to bring SURGE back to store shelves everywhere." (Their emphasis, not ours.) Twenty-eight people have been inducted, including Drew Bizell. The aspiring film student produced "Save Surge—the Movie," a 28-minute documentary of his quest to find the beverage in his hometown of Bryan, Texas. (Alas, he did not.) The SaveSurge Hall of Fame might not be what most people put on their professional résumés, but the recognition it provides goes a long way toward fulfilling a promise of community ownership.

If you think Karkovack and his carbonated band of soda activists don't fit mainstream expectations of how people spend their free time, you're right. Some might call them the lunatic fringe. The traditions of mass consumption and mass media, where averages rule and the edges do not, would eject the SaveSurgians as a statistical anomaly. Karkovack is aware of the dismissals but isn't bowed by them. "I would say they are wrong. These people are passionate about your product. Why would you ever ignore them or refer to them in a derogatory way? I think you can learn a lot from your customers. I think Coke has learned a lot from our group."

That may be as far as the Surge activists get. In May 2005, Coca-Cola began test-marketing Vault. Billed as a citrus "hybrid energy soda," Vault also hailed from the alien-green family of soda colors that seem to appeal to teenage boys and young men. When he first learned of its existence, Karkovack drove four hours south to Virginia to buy a case, only to find that the beverage had not yet arrived in stores. Before his expedition, Karkovack had contacted the local bottler to ensure Vault would be available. It showed up in the stores the following day. He made the four-hour trip home sans Vault.

"The benefit was that I came home and complained about it on the SaveSurge blog. Someone from Coke read that and decided to send me a whole slew of Vault and related items: three cases of the soda, a little grill with the Vault logo on it, T-shirts, hats, and an inflatable bottle. It turned out better than if I had found it in Virginia the first time."

Blind taste tests of the beverages conducted by the community found that few could tell the difference. That convinced most of the community that Vault was Surge reincarnated, and Save-Surgians embraced it as a worthy substitute. It was an inspirational moment. "We were getting an influx of e-mails from people about Vault, sending in reviews and pictures. It didn't fit with *SaveSurge.org* so we decided to start new again and have a site dedicated to Vault and Vault only. We tied the communities together by keeping the same bulletin board and e-mail newsletter. We find that Surge and Vault fans are pretty much one and the same." That means Coke fumbled its stewardship of Surge and spent a bundle to rebrand essentially the same product.

In June 2005, undaunted by Coke's apparent disregard to resurrect Surge, Karkovack built and launched a new fan site: *VaultKicks.org*. Its purpose: "To do our part to ensure the success of Vault in its test-marketing and to lobby Coca-Cola to launch Vault nationwide." When Vault started showing up in test markets, Karkovack's community heated up. Coke paid attention. "After the test-marketing, we were starting to see in the traffic reports for our Web site that there were a lot of people from Coke visiting our site on a daily basis." It may have been enough to help Coke finalize its decision; the company launched Vault nationally in January 2006 just as they did with Surge: with Super Bowl commercials.

While Karkovack was busy with the VaultKicks Web site, Coca-Cola fully armed Vault to conquer the market owned by

Mountain Dew. It planned "an integrated marketing campaign, including television, radio, outdoor and print advertising, as well as point-of-sale advertising." An interesting approach given that Vault's ideal audience was abandoning traditional media outlets. A 2003 study by Yahoo and Carat North America found that in an average week, teens and young adults aged 13 to 24 spent more time online (16.7 hours to be exact, not including time spent with e-mail) than they did watching TV (13.6 hours). If the ideal Vault drinkers were at all like Karkovack and his community of 1,000 soda lovers, then they were more likely to be Web savvy and hanging out in front of the computer screen, not the television screen. Nearly ten years separated the Surge and Vault launches, and the media-consumption patterns for the products' ideal customers had changed substantially. Coke was fully armed for battle but charging toward the wrong battlefield.

Twelve months after launching *VaultKicks.org* with no official recognition from Coke, Karkovack registered 969 fans, who had posted 29,428 articles. A search for "Vault soda" on Google in 2006 returned *VaultKicks.org* as the top search result. The number two result was *SaveSurge.org*. The site Coca-Cola created for Vault, *drinkvault.com,* didn't show up in the first 25 pages of Google search results. That made *VaultKicks.org* the de facto Web site for the beverage. "There's really not a whole lot on *drinkvault.com,"* Karkovak says. "People are actually finding our Web site in Google first when they search for Vault. It's kinda neat to think that we are ahead of Coke on this.

"I think they [Coca-Cola] have a lot to learn about interactive marketing. They obviously have done a lot with television, radio, and print, but their web marketing has been a step below that. They haven't done much of anything. You look at most of their product Web sites; they are never updated. They are basically just static information, and there's really no way for people who are fans to get in contact with the company and tell them 'Good job; we enjoy your product.'" With Vault came a reality—it was time to reevaluate the purpose of SaveSurge. The community was already being transferred to VaultKicks. The fans are doing for free what a company would normally do itself.

Companies that find themselves with a group of Karkovacks on their radar are clearly failing at a fundamental skill: "Listening. Listen to your customers. See what they are doing online. Take it to heart. If someone is saying something negative about you or something that they want you to do, you really should consider it because these are the people who make your company what it is. If you don't have a passionate customer base, you're not going to have much of a brand left in a few years."

"I think it's going to be difficult in the future for companies because they are going to have to find staff to watch over these things. They are going to have to find ways to interact with their fans. That's one thing that Coke has done a little bit since we have been involved with them. It has found ways to be a little more consumer-friendly. It has put more info on its Web site. The folks at the 800 number and e-mail help center have a lot more information now. I think Coke has empowered its employees a little more. Coke was notorious for sending cease-and-desist letters to fan clubs back in the late 1990s," said Karkovack. "Rather than threatening legal action, the more productive thing would be to reach a hand out to these people and say, 'What can we do to make things better?' If a company takes time to speak with you about your concerns, it means a lot more to the consumer than sending a 500-page cease-and-desist order. It's a whole new era."

SaveSurge has become a model for people lobbying to save other brands and commercial properties. A group of fans hoping to save the television show *Angel* from cancellation asked

Karkovack if they could model their lobbying campaign on his. "When we started the Web site, there weren't a lot of sites out there dedicated to saving anything. And now they seem to pop up every hour." Karkovack's advice for fellow product activists: "Don't give up. I had people from Coke tell me in the beginning that our Web site was nice, but it's not going to do anything." He is firm about being polite. Threats and juvenilia are counterproductive. Be honest. Ensure you present yourself and your community well. Write intelligent letters. Ensure flawless spelling. "If they think you are an intelligent, well-spoken person with a little money to spend, they will listen."

Despite Coke's behind-the-curve effort with the online presence of Vault, how would he grade the company's efforts now? "I'd give them a solid B. Back when we started, it would have been a D or an F. They have come around. They allowed us to be the first Web site in the country to announce the Vault national launch. They have gone from ignoring us completely to wanting us to spill their big news to everyone, so that's a big step forward for them." Plus, it's free labor. The grassroots nature of Karkovack's work may not equal a marketing campaign in 920,000 convenience stores, but that's not the purpose of citizen marketers. Their focus is often an attempt to transcend brand awareness into action by creating amateur networks of affiliation. One step toward action is to grant those who seek it the ownership they crave. Karkovack's years-long work with what is essentially a hobby means that *VaultKicks.org* is unlikely to suffer from inattention. "I am definitely going to keep it around for a long time," he said. "One of the lessons we learned from Surge was that you can't take something for granted while you have it because it could be gone before you know it."

~

Sociologists and historians might call the work of Karkovack "productive leisure." Productive leisure bridges our work lives and our home lives while validating our role as workers in a free and capitalistic market. It confirms who we are and what we do. That's the thesis advanced by Steven M. Gelber, a cultural historian at Santa Clara University in Silicon Valley. He examined the history of hobbyists in a scholarly book on the subject called *Hobbies: Leisure and the Culture of Work in America.*

"Hobbies are important because they combine critical and affirmative elements [and are] a way to confirm the verities of work and the free market inside the home so long as remunerative employment has remained elsewhere," he writes. They exercise our creative minds and our capitalist imaginations. That means hobbies are fun, productive, and meaningful . . . just as long as a paycheck supports them.

Of the several types of popular hobbies, one citizen marketer has a peculiar one: collecting Starbucks. His name is Winter (which he claims is his new legal name), and he's a Houston-based freelance computer programmer who spends his leisure time trying to visit every Starbucks store ever opened in the world. He began his quixotic quest in 1998 and eight years later he has visited 5,729 stores in seven countries, which he chronicles on his Web site. He orders a half-filled tall espresso from each store, chugs it down, and sprints, literally, to the next one on his list. Why? "Part of it is my collector's instinct," he says. "Once I get into collecting things, I have to have it all. I'm big into comic books, cards, and coins. Essentially I'm collecting these Starbucks. And I'm compelled by my instinct to get them all." The inevitable stories about him reaffirm the ubiquitous and, arguably, culturally reaffirming role that Starbucks fulfills for parts of society, not to mention its overall consistency. "The coffee is amazingly consistent, even overseas," he says.

If we explore the rationale for collecting, Gelber says, mass production "democratized collecting by creating objects whose very commonness assured they would become scarce because they were usually made to be thrown away. Hobby collectors rescued objects from the trash heap and created value by inventing sets into which to fit them." As a collector, Winter succinctly catalogs each of his Starbucks experiences in his laptop. He is a collector of meaning in a way that perhaps few, if any, other people would collect. His hobby collects attention, too. The publicity is not always in a format Starbucks would like: "After about four stores, the coffee loses all taste," says Winter, who is unconcerned about any long-term effects of so much coffee. "After an extreme number of stores, I have to wash out the taste with water after every sip because it's starting to make me sick."

Despite his not-always-happy-face for Starbucks, Winter is the message. Starbucks is important enough to him to visit every one in the world. His collector's quest is authentic (and expensive); therefore, he is the message. That's a bitter brew for companies insistent on neat, consistent, and always-positive messaging. Everyone knows that nothing is perfect, yet companies persist in portraying their perfection. That's why authenticity is magnetic—it's truth made real. When everyone has the potential to publish and broadcast, the day-to-day stories of their lives, in all of its various forms, it contributes to the collective human experience in all of its various idiosyncrasies. Just as Justin Hall lived his life out loud and online, so too do the Winters of the world. Some are more attached to products and brands than others. Their resultant hobby journalism is bound to affect the image managers of the world in ways they neither expect or desire. Starbucks is consistently polite about Winter's quest, but it's also terse about it, maybe dismissive. "We are flattered by Winter's enthusiasm for the Starbucks experience," said a spokesperson, "and we wish him well with his endeavors." When *U.S.News & World Report* asked McDonald's about the citizen-marketer work of the McChronicles blogger, a company spokesperson would only say that blogs are "a valuable communications tool" and that "we appreciate that customers who relate to our brand are sharing their thoughts about McDonald's with others." These two mechanized responses continue to portray the company-as-monolith, not as an organization staffed by real people with authentic regard for their sometimes quirky customers. They are marginalizing the 1 Percenters.

It wasn't until about 1880 that hobbies were considered culturally acceptable. As the world transitioned from an agrarian culture to an industrialist one, it created a natural division between work and leisure. In the agrarian culture, work and home life were one and the same. But as the manufacturing industry grew and industrialism took over, work was hardly creative or intellectually stimulating for the masses. That spurred the growth of hobbyism. As Professor Gelber explains, "Hobbies gained wide acceptance because they could condemn depersonalized factory and office work by compensating for its deficits while simultaneously replicating both the skills and the values of the workplace." He calls this process "disguised affirmation," and it grants participants the permission to consider an activity recreation while it works subconsciously as ideological re-creation. As we shape our tools, our tools shape us, Marshall McLuhan reminds us, and then we become what we behold. With the right tools, a hobbyist imagines the world as it could or as it should be. That could certainly explain the work of our Fanatics—their work is often to encourage word of mouth *and* fulfill their lofty expectations. Or to simply be "awesome," as McChronicles defined it.

~

The quest to save Surge and Barq's, promote Vault and Disney, help TiVo, and glorify Apple and all of the other brands we've mentioned so far is what marketing academics have called "market helping behavior." It describes the behavior of everyday people who help one another with decisions on what to buy and who to buy it from. In research extending back to the 1960s, researchers began to confirm and quantify what most of us take for granted today. Throughout the 1960s, 1970s, and 1980s, when companies could often buy their way to growth through extensive advertising campaigns, marketing researchers found that 40 percent of a retailer's clientele was typically based on the recommendations of other people. One study from the 1980s found that 9 out of 10 people relied on a friend's opinion when buying a durable product, like a washing machine or air conditioner. That same study found that 21 percent of people would rely on strangers or a friend of a friend of a friend for product information and advice.

If hobbyism is the form, what is the function? Why do people involve themselves in market-helping behaviors? There are four reasons: altruism, personal relevance, common good, and status.

Altruism and empathy are siblings. A volunteer on TiVo-Community helps solve the problem of a fellow TiVo user because he feels bad about the other's poor experience. Because of their natures, some people cannot stand to see others grappling with problems or having a bad time. Their Good Samaritanism is manifested by participating in a forum like TiVoCommunity or TreoCentral. Whether it's nature or nurture, citizen marketers often feel the need to give something to others. It's certainly a virtue of Americans that observers of history have documented. When he spent nine months traveling across the United States in

1831, the aristocratic Frenchman Alexis de Tocqueville found an America rich with bourgeoisie virtue—a desire to help one another with teaching, governing, and building communities. He found Americans demonstrated a natural desire to meet and create "associations." He wrote: "Americans of all ages, all stations of life, and all types of disposition are forever forming associations. . . . In democratic countries knowledge of how to combine is the mother of all other forms of knowledge; on its progress depends that of all the others." They formed associations because America then was a vast and uncultivated country. America's early citizens had to stick together to survive their pioneering ventures. That helped dispel the class distinctions so prevalent in Old World Europe. It was strength of character, not family lineage, that rallied people toward common goals. Industriousness was the prevailing ethic, and that extended into the governance of life. "In towns it is impossible to prevent men from assembling, getting excited together and forming sudden passionate resolves," he wrote. "Towns are like great meeting houses with all the inhabitants as members. In them the people wield immense influence over their magistrates and often carry their desires into execution without intermediaries."

Personal relevance drives citizen marketers because a product, brand, company, or person has lit their creative fuse. When they launch a blog or Web site devoted to discussing or promoting a brand or company, it is a vehicle for their conceptualization of self. All of the citizen marketers we spoke with emphasized how their individual icons of devotion provide meaning. It's the beginning of affinity, a relationship that feeds their enduring involvement. The subtext underlying the work of citizen marketers is that "this brand is relevant to me." That relevance is attractive to others who feel a similar intuition. "They are people who are affirming the meaning of products and companies and merely making their worlds integrated," Gelber explained during a conversation we had about citizen marketers. "To them, the company is a living totem. It represents them and helps keep their spirit alive."

Common good is the driver for the devoted contributors to Wikipedia. For their own personal reasons, they think the world can be a better place and contribute toward that goal. The use of the word *world* is somewhat relative because not everyone benefits from an article about the rock band Blink 182, for instance. The common good means contributing, cooperating, or improving the community. People who do not pick up after their dogs subtract from the common good of everyone who uses the park more than people who simply stroll through it. They are the park's freeloaders, ignorant of or willfully flouting their responsibility toward the common good. But the freeloaders can be stopped. Scientists in England and Germany discovered in 2005 that sanctions against freeloaders, even if delivered by a few people, improve the overall fortunes of a group. The experiment involved 84 people whose individual goal was to make as much money as possible. Participants were divided into two teams—the first one depended on voluntary cooperation, and the second one allowed its members to sanction those who didn't cooperate. A sanction wasn't free—it cost money. Very quickly, people in the sanctioning group were making more money in the experiment than the other group because more of them contributed toward the group's success, especially in the pooling of funds. Their contribution cost them in the short term but produced better returns in the long run. Furthermore, the "freeloaders" in the first group eventually switched to the sanctioning group, and they began to punish others who didn't cooperate. "Despite initial aversion, the entire population migrates successively to the sanctioning institution and strongly cooperates, whereas the sanction-free society becomes fully depopulated," the authors of the study wrote. Promoting the common good is the goal of democracy because of its nature of distributed power and guarantee of liberty. Those who violate its principles by breaking its rule of law are punished for the common good of the public. In reality, however, the common good is relative in a democratic society, where wealth and property are the domains of the individual. Thus, tangible common goods are unevenly distributed.

Status is the natural human driver of success. Unless we are laid up sick and incapacitated, status often drives purchases, jobs, neighborhood improvements, and our own sense of self-worth. Market-helping behaviors reaffirm or improve one's value to social networks. Status improves our chances of making connections and finding success. As outwardly friendly people, citizen marketers are typically well connected. They have strong networks to which they attend. They are often like Armand Frasco. From his home in Niles, Illinois, he was describing a call he'd received one day out of the blue.

"Hello-ah, Aramando," he said, using his best imitation of an Italian accent. "It's ah-Francesco Franceschi!"

Franceschi was calling from Milan, Italy. He was co-owner of Modo & Modo, maker of Moleskine, a decidedly nontechnical, richly traditional notebook favored by designers and artists. Franceschi was calling because Frasco had built a following with Moleskinerie, a blog that he started on a whim one day in 2004. The several hours per day Frasco devoted to Moleskinerie was now attracting about 5,000 visitors per day. As a Fanatic for Moleskine, Frasco encouraged visitors to share their stories about the small black notebook that decades earlier had been the journal and sketchpad of choice for Vincent Van Gogh, Henri Matisse, and Ernest Hemingway. (In the 4 *F*s model, Frasco is a Fanatic.)

Franceschi was also calling because Moleskinerie had spawned copycat fan sites around the world, nine in all, and most of them in languages other than English. Like Moleskinerie, all are maintained by people independent of the company. By most accounts, they are essentially the notebook's only organized global marketing.

"I thought, well, I have a Typepad account, and I have a Moleskine. What happens if I combine the two?" is how Frasco recalls his decision to launch Moleskinerie. Franceschi, along with a partner, had revived what was essentially a dead brand. A French company had owned Moleskine previously, but inattention and neglect slowly killed it. So Franceschi partnered with Mario Baruzzi and bought Moleskine in 1998. They set out to re-create the magic that inevitably follows in the draft of the world's most famous artists. By deftly focusing on exceptional manufacturing quality and a few obvious but killer features (a black elastic band wraps around the outside to hold the French-vanilla-colored pages of the notebook closed tightly), the Italian entrepreneurs used Moleskine's history as its distinct selling advantage. That helped it become a cult product with main-stream sales numbers: 4.5 million Moleskines were sold in 2005. Most marketing was being done by volunteers like Frasco, who works by day as a commercial photographer. In August 2006, Modo & Modo cashed out; they sold Moleskine to a French company for 60 million euros. The sale marked yet another interesting chapter in the history of Moleskine; not only was the company sold back to the French but it illustrated a parable about redemption, of how a brand that was once considered dead was given new life by a 13-person company that focused on the notebook's magical past and the volunteerism of its most passion-ate fans, its citizen marketers.

Those citizen marketers are scattered around the world. For several years, they have worked on behalf of Moleskine because it is a rally point for their own personal work. They facilitate discussions and launch projects that feature the notebook. A very active

Flickr community documents the art they create in their Moleskines. Perched in the center of that world of fans is Armand Frasco. So why a fan blog dedicated to, of all things, a notebook? After all, it does not come in trendy colors or extol techie features like GPS, much less a sleeve for a compact disc. It's sold primarily in one color: black. Henry Ford would approve of its old-school focus.

"I feel deeply responsible for the product. Why? I don't know," Frasco said, and then paused for a long moment. "Because I feel like, since I own the product, I don't want to damage it. I want to help. You see, I've always liked travel. I listened to shortwave radio when I was a kid. You close your eyes, and you're there. As a documentary photographer, I want to help people document their lives. So with this site, I'm helping people document their lives. That may sound trivial to many people, but it's not to me." Plus there's the Moleskine history by artistic association. "There's a magic associated with it, and people want to believe it," he said.

When the true believers or the curious search for Moleskine on Google, Moleskinerie is often the third or fourth result. That's one reason why Franceschi started calling Frasco regularly: a highly ranked fan site can be a key source of influence. According to Frasco, his blog has value for Modo & Modo: "We're like an informal focus group, and that's a huge advantage for them."

Although Franceschi could have monitored the blog anonymously, Frasco said Franceschi preferred a personal connection. Both obviously relished the connection, especially Frasco: "We share a lot of beliefs." Plus it's more efficient to take a barometer reading of a brand's health directly from the weatherman in the field, not from a weather Web site. "Corporations should realize the power of a community," Frasco said. Modo & Modo did, which fueled Frasco's concentration on Moleskinerie.

"I feel like there's a partnership between us, and that's grati-fying," Frasco recalls of his talks with Franceschi. "We don't talk about the business side of Moleskine. We talk about issues of the world, and that's very profound to me." Now that Moleskine is in the hands of a new owner, the big question for Frasco and all of the other Moleskine volunteer marketers is "how they will deal with us."

"I hope Mr. Franceschi will put out a good word for us, better yet, shepherd the same support with the new owners. I have a feeling he's that kind of person."

There's something about people doing dumb things in front of a video camera that captures the cultural interest and imagi-nations of many people. But what is it? Why is our culture trans-fixed by what the critic George Will calls "sophisticated delivery of stupidity"? Our attempt to answer this question turns us toward Japan.

In the mid-1980s, Ken Shimura and Cha Kato hosted a pop-ular Japanese television show that lampooned Japanese society and its icons. One segment of the show capitalized on the growing number of portable video cameras in Japanese households. The hosts invited viewers to send their own homemade videos to the show, where the hosts would play them and, of course, gleefully ridicule them. Vin Di Bona was an American television producer at the time and saw the show. He liked it, so he purchased rights to repackage it for American television audiences. He dumped the skits and the dual-host format in favor of an entire program about home movies created by viewers. *America's Funniest Home Videos* (more affectionately known as *AFHV*) debuted on January 14,

1990, on ABC. Within three months, it was the number-one ranked television series in America.

AFHV was not George Will material. It was puppies and babies acting up and captured accidents on sidewalks and in back-yards. Most of it was slapstick comedy, as performed by amateurs. Part of the appeal was the potential to participate. No talent required, just the luck necessary to catch or create a funny moment on videotape and mail it to ABC, where it would join 2,000 videotapes the show was receiving each day. Ad parodies and lip-synching videos were favorites, but events rigged to look accidental or spontaneous were tossed. The show's producers cited humor as the linchpin; people who could laugh at themselves and culture and invite others to laugh with them simultaneously made it all insignificant, harmless fun.

AFHV was still on ABC in 2006; that made it the third-long-est running primetime show for the network after *20/20* and *Primetime.* But in 2006, *AFHV* was being challenged by video-sharing sites where any citizen in the world could upload their funniest video. For instance, here is how we would describe an online citizen marketer video created by two twentysomething men that is an "ad" for McDonald's Chicken McNuggets.

The scene is daytime. Outside. Spring. The sky is clear. Two young men are in the frame. On the left is Fernando Sosa, 25. His dark hair is well-groomed; he's wearing a dark hooded sweatshirt whose sleeves fall several inches past his hands. To the right of Fernando is Thomas Middleditch, 24. He is taller and sandy blond. He is wearing very large sunglasses and a blue and white tracksuit jacket. In the background, we can see Wrigley Field, home of major league baseball's Chicago Cubs, and a McDonald's. Cars can be seen and heard driving down a nearby street. The video begins. Fernando is a human beatbox as Thomas raps:

"I'm into Nuggets, y'all, I'm into Nuggets, y'all.
I'm into Nuggets, y'all. I'm into Nuggets, y'all."

For another 30 seconds, Thomas raps repetitively about "ketchup and mayo" and dipping McNuggets "in that BBQ sauce!" It's funny and innocuous, and the "music" for this citizen ad has an insanely infectious melody that tends to stick in the listener's head. It is also popular. Adding up the number of views on several video-sharing sites, "I'm into Nuggets Y'all" has been watched nearly 100,000 times.

Sosa and Middleditch are friends who met as students at the Conservatory Program at Chicago's famed Second City. One March night in 2006, while waiting to go onstage to perform their schoolwork, Sosa was munching on a preshow snack of McNuggets. That inspired Middleditch to call up his hip-hop "urban character" and improvise a rap. Sosa chimed in with some beatbox beats. The show's director was nearby and loved the impromptu performance. He asked them to perform it as the show's opener. The crowed cheered. The director and other Second City instructors did too and recommended they record it as a short video for their portfolios. With a film-savvy friend behind the camera, they shot the video in 20 minutes near Wrigley Field and edited it as an ode to Chicken McNuggets. Friends posted it to video sharing sites YouTube and *StupidVideos.com*.

We met up with them at Middleditch's Lakeview neighborhood apartment on the north side of Chicago and talked in the back room next to the foosball table while two French bulldogs locked away in his bedroom cried for attention. Sosa says reactions to their video ranged from "I hate it, but I can't stop watching it" to "I love it, and I can't stop watching it." One friend told him she bought McNuggets because she found herself singing the song while ordering.

Middleditch calls it "the most retarded thing I've ever created," creating an irony to the story: they are critical of McDonald's. "I try to stay away from it; it's pretty bad for you," Middleditch says. "I feel bad when I hear that kind of stuff happening," Middleditch says of people buying McNuggets because of their infectious jingle. "I helped this big evil corporation out— for free. Oh, it's so bad. So, there you go McDonald's."

Sosa feigns disgust. "We helped line their pockets."

Their contempt for the world's largest restaurant company lies in efforts to affect culture, not reflect it. Both are prime potential customers, but they consider the company's efforts to appeal to them as patronizing and out of touch. "I feel like McDonald's is trying to connect with people, but they don't get it," Middleditch says. "McDonald's wants to be cool, but it's like 50-year-old guys *trying* to be cool." He quickly takes on the visage of Stuffy Middle-Aged Businessman. "This is cool, right? It's cool to be like this. Am I right, guys? OK, cool. Wow, I said it: 'cool!'"

"That's what I feel like McDonald's is trying to do with all their ads and the 'ba da da da da,'" Middleditch says, as he segues into the company's "I'm Lovin' It" jingle. "Like they are so hip, but it is so contrived and so far off base. Very little of what I think is good or what I would promote to friends is based on upon the advertising you give me. Today, I went to eat at Subway and a kid, it must have been his first day, was saying, 'Eat fresh!' to everyone after he rang them through. 'Thanks for coming to Subway. Eat fresh!' It was really funny. No one would ever say something like that! I wouldn't go to a Subway thinking 'Oh, this is going to be eating fresh.' I just think, 'This is not a greasy burger, and it tastes pretty good.'"

Neither have marketing experience or selling backgrounds (Middleditch is a dog walker and Sosa works at an accounting firm), and they were a bit baffled by our interest in talking with them about McDonald's and citizen marketing, but their natural inclination as canny observers and reflectors of pop culture leads them to believe that companies should partner with the people they're trying to reach.

"They are spending so much money with the commercials they are doing now," Sosa says of the big brands. "We spent like a dollar on the McNuggets themselves. In 20 minutes, for barely any cost, we had the video." Middleditch jumps in: "If you want to target a certain audience, get someone from that audience and bring them on board. Even if it is just for that project. If I see a commercial that looks as if it is *trying* to appeal to me, I want to vomit." Our conversation with the guys ended appropriately enough; Middleditch had work to do. The bulldogs had peed on his bed.

Sosa and Middleditch represent the future of citizen content creators and citizen marketers. They are "millennials," young men and women born after 1982. They are highly adept with digital tools not only because their baby boomer parents bought them computers and cell phones but because they often are doing video editing work and mashups in school media labs. They are sophisticated students of audio and video. Because of their familiarity with the tools, and because they tend to reject the "extreme" individualism of the Gen Xers who preceded them, the millennials are the generation most likely to have the biggest impact on participatory culture. That's the argument advanced by William Strauss and Neil Howe in their brilliant work, *Millennials and the Pop Culture.*

They are actively promoting the democratization of the pop culture. Many teens are patching together software that allows them to produce their own songs, movies, or programs. They enjoy sharing their creations or discoveries with each other, and they naturally prefer to do this with few or no commercial intermediaries. Millennials perceive strongly in their sense of mastery over how technology can be applied to pop culture. . . . For most youths, the pop culture—buying it, creating it, downloading it, manipulating it, sharing it—is where the pieces come together at the center of a *whole new lifestyle*.

Strauss and Howe have sufficiently described our McDonald's rappers as well as many of the twentysomething citizen marketers and citizen content creators we spoke with. The millennials want to interact with culture. That's what they expect having grown up with TiVo, cell phones, and video games that put them in control. Passive TV or movie watching is far less interesting than interacting with media. Or creating it. Give them control or they'll probably find something else to do. A good starting point is to start turning control over to them with a vote, a voice, and a connection.

The Power of One

The hero is the champion of things becoming,
not of things become.

Joseph Campbell, *The Hero with a Thousand Faces*

Despite what he did, Casey Neistat really is a fan of Apple Computer. As a multimedia artist, he uses almost every kind of Apple equipment imaginable, from his Macintosh computer to his Apple Cinema Display to his small iPod music player. When his iPod conked out, what he did wasn't friendly to the company. He created enough attention that die-hard Apple loyalists "were panicking because they [felt] like we might cause somebody to not buy a Macintosh."

Neistat was 22 and living in New York City. He had purchased a first-generation iPod in early 2002, not long after Apple first introduced the portable music player. After 18 months of daily use and after the warranty expired, the rechargeable lithium-ion battery wouldn't charge anymore. He called Apple's technical support number. They could fix the iPod, but it would cost $255 plus a mail-in fee, almost equal to the cost of a new machine. An employee at an Apple retail store in Manhattan told him the same thing.

What was he supposed to do? Fixing his iPod was expensive, almost equal to the cost of buying a new one. That wasn't money Neistat had lying around his apartment to replace a dead iPod. "I felt taken advantage of and exploited," he said later. It was as if Apple were selling iPods as expensive yet disposable toys. Neistat's older brother, Van, also a longtime Apple fan, "thought this was really un-Apple. Something has to be done. Somebody has to speak up."

One day, they were standing in front of a row of large, brightly colored iPod posters. That's when the idea hit: hack the posters. They created a stencil that read, "iPod's Unreplaceable Battery Only Lasts 18 Months." They spray painted the stencil over dozens of posters dotting the city. Van filmed Casey doing it. They called Apple support again and recorded the call. Same answer as before: $255, plus a mail-in fee, to replace the battery. There was this kicker, too: "At that price, you may as well just go buy a new one." They mashed this quote into a video they called "iPod's Dirty Secret." They posted the video to their Web site and notified 30 friends, who sent it to their friends. Within six weeks, the video had been downloaded over a million times.

It was everywhere on the Internet and traditional media— more than 130 news outlets from around the world, including the *Washington Post*, the *Daily Yomiuri* in Japan, the *China Post*, and the BBC featured the story. *Rolling Stone* proclaimed it the "Apple Backlash." Then Apple called.

"Good news," the company caller said. Apple had a new battery replacement program. For out-of-warranty iPods, it would replace the battery for a $99 fee. (Apple later reduced it to $59.) "My first question was, 'Are you calling me in response to the film that we made?'" Casey said. "Their response to that was,

'We can neither confirm nor deny that we have seen that film.'" (Apple said the battery-replacement offer had been in the works for months.)

The Neistat brothers had used Apple's famously powerful and easy-to-learn tools against Apple, proving that no one—not even the Apple mother ship—is immune to a backlash launched by a single customer, or duo of brothers. Considering the obvious and plentiful media attention the brothers had attained for their Firecracker ad (they called it a "public service announcement"), Apple's odd response—"we can neither confirm nor deny"—was not one of its better moments. The guerilla work of the Neistat brothers paved the way for future customer protests employing easy-to-use multimedia tools and the inherent word-of-mouth of social media.

What caused "iPod's Dirty Secret," "Dell Hell," and a dozen of the other citizen-created Firecracker ads to catch on? Why do things spread? One explanation is the *meme,* a cultural transmitter that distinguishes an idea from the billions of others that float in the primordial soup of daily human existence. The evolutionary theorist Richard Dawkins coined the term in his book *The Selfish Gene.*

"Just as genes propagate themselves in the gene pool by leaping from body to body via sperms or eggs, so memes propagate themselves in the meme pool by leaping from brain to brain via a process which, in the broad sense, can be called imitation," states Dawkins. "Examples of memes are tunes, catchphrases, clothes fashions, and ways of making pots or of building arches." We can extend that to include concepts, ideas, theories, opinions, beliefs, practices, habits, and dances (Macarena, anyone?) that propagate in a culture. What makes the work of citizen marketers important is that broadband and social media tools expedite the spread of memes. That's good news for someone with a catchy idea.

One reason why citizen-created memes spread is that they often follow the four stages of successful meme replication:

1. Assimilation. The meme is noticed, understood, and accepted by someone, who becomes a host of the meme.

2. Retention. It's embedded in memory. The longer it's stored there, the better.

3. Expression. The idea can take some form, such as language, text, pictures, or in even in unconscious behavior, such as the way someone walks.

4. Transmission. The host passes the meme on to one or more people.

To better understand the science, we can look at how the Neistat brothers' "iPod's Dirty Secret" video spread. To be assimilated, a meme must be noticed, understood, and accepted by the host. "iPod's Dirty Secret" was first assimilated by the online community of rabid Apple users. Given that there were about 1.4 million iPods in use at the time, early recipients of the meme probably owned an iPod, too, and understood that the battery cannot be changed easily, if at all, by the average person.

Retention depends on how important the idea is to the host and how often it is repeated. Apple has long been known to have a cultlike following, cultivated over 30 years of producing highly stylized computer equipment. Many Apple fans eagerly consume news or rumors about the company and its products. With so many Apple forums online, the "Dirty Secret" meme quickly ping-ponged through blogs and discussion boards. Citizen marketers have a clear advantage for expression: the Neistat brothers' video is very creative. On top of a hip-hop soundtrack, it mixes audio from Apple's call-center technician with footage from Casey stenciling posters all over New York. The video is surprising and something that iPod owners would probably pass on to other iPod-owning friends. The transmission signal for the "Dirty Secret" video was the brothers' Web site. The signal was spread first by iPod users and Apple fans online and then to other interested parties around the world. Traditional media, including print and television, picked up the story and amplified it.

Here's another story that followed the four stages of meme replication and spread from person to person. In the summer of 2006, Brian Finkelstein's Comcast Internet connection kept dying. It took several calls to have someone take a look, but a technician arrived to replace the broadband modem of the Washington, D.C., law student. When the technician dialed the company's support line to activate the replacement modem, he was put on hold. For 90 minutes. While the technician was on hold, he fell asleep on Finkelstein's couch.

It's not a normal occurrence for a technician to fall asleep on your couch. This unlucky technician did, mostly because his own company put him on hold for 90 minutes. Powerless to do much else, what else is there to do? That was of little concern to Finkelstein, of course. He did what any media-savvy law student would do: he grabbed his video camera. He filmed the technician, decked out in a red Comcast golf shirt and khaki shorts, zonked out on the couch with a laptop balanced on his knee. In the age of social media and YouTube, the most popular videos are music videos. Finkelstein paired the footage of the sleeping tech to a song by the Eels called "I Need Some Sleep." Screens of text read: "Thanks, Comcast, for two broken routers, four hour appointment blocks, weeklong Internet outages, long hold times, high prices, three missed appointments. Thanks for everything." He posted it to *YouTube.com* and mentioned it on his blog. The word of mouth jetstream powered by bloggers swooped it up and sent it around the world. Two weeks later, the video had been viewed 200,000 times. The story was picked up all of the traditional media and international news agencies. A month later, the video had been viewed 750,000 times.

The day after Finkelstein posted his video, a regional vice president at Comcast called. He was going to come by with a team of technicians and fix the problem himself. With a focus on damage control, Comcast announced the sleeping technician had been fired. But it was too late. Frustrated Comcast customers vented their anger about similar stories on blogs and online communities. It was the Jeff Jarvis experience all over again, this time starring a different company. With the Power of One, Google never forgets. News outlets do, as they must, but Google does not. Google had captured the story, the outrage, and the reaction, and will catalog it indefinitely for customers, prospects, and business historians. You are your Google results.

Not everyone will have the time, ability, or imagination to record a customer-service problem gone wrong. But the 1 Percenters do. Because of their creativity and familiarity with multimedia tools, the outlaws don't care. In a study that Nielsen BuzzMetrics conducted of people who create content online, it discovered that they are more likely to have high-speed Internet connections, cell phones, MP3 players, digital cameras, laptops, and TiVos or other DVRs than people who don't create content online. The younger the age, the more technologically advanced they seem to be. That describes Brian Finkelstein and the Neistat brothers.

From the stories of Jeff Jarvis's Dell Hell, Vincent Ferrari's call with AOL, the Neistat brothers' iPod experience, and Brian Finkelstein's sleeping Comcast technician, we learn that a well-designed meme can spread considerably faster with the aid of social media. A meme spreads, typically, because it matches the experiences of others and exposes a truth. Wronged citizen marketers will lash out on their blogs, in forums, and, as we've seen, in homemade short videos that then become commercials for companies' wrongdoings. With the foundations of a meme in place, what are the mechanics of its spread among social media?

1. Bloggers spread a story that has a surprising development. A technician sleeping on the couch is about as surprising as they come.

2. The story is filled with numerous and concrete details. If the story includes audio, video, or photographic evidence, its chances of spreading increase significantly.

3. The story documents a tangible form of injustice. Multiple missed appointments, a belligerent customer service rep, and so forth.

4. The story reaches a plateau of recognition among a number of well-known blogs. It may show up as a top search term on Technorati or the front page of Digg. When it makes the big Filter sites, that often triggers the interest of the traditional media. Within several days to a week, newspapers write a story about the incident. Within one to five days after that, one or several broadcast media outlets create a story.

5. The story reaches a worldwide plateau. Within hours or days of the story hitting the mainstream media, someone posts the video of the broadcast story to YouTube, fueling its spread. Many of the original bloggers post regular updates tracking the story's progress.

With today's tools and the right motivation, an everyday person has a much better chance of creating a scene about a company or product experience than ever before. The customers have more control. Caveat venditor. Let the seller beware.

July 27, 2005, was a memorable day for a certain 28-year old married mother of one in Albany, New York. *Forbes* magazine had just named her month-old Web site, Slave to Target, as "Best Shopping Blog" in its annual Web awards. It was also the day she thought a $52 billion company was calling to sue her. The caller ID said Target Corp., so it only made sense in her mind that an angry official from the retailer was calling with the news that an expensive and embarrassing lawsuit was imminent followed by fines and sanctions, all because of her blog. They were probably angry her blog featured handcuffs wrapped around Target's iconic red bulls-eye. But she didn't know about the *Forbes* recognition. She didn't know it was sending her gobs of Web visitors. She didn't know that what she would do next would be a big mistake.

Without listening to the voice mail and in one panic-filled click of a mouse button, she deleted her blog. A month's worth of Target evangelism vanished. Then she listened to the voice mail. A Target marketing manager named John—she can't remember his last name—was calling.

"Oh my god! I'm so excited! Did you see *Forbes?*" John cried into the voice mail. He had tracked her down through her Target affiliate link, which rewards Web site operators who link to products on *Target.com.* Relieved and laughing at herself, she started all over again.

On her blog, and in her chat with us, she remains anonymous. She is nervous about revealing her identity because she sometimes writes snarky and racy things about Target and its products, many of which she loves and describes as if she'd had a glass of wine or two. She worries her raciness may reflect poorly on her clients (she says she is the proprietor of a public-relations firm for independent designers). We worry she may be an *astroturfer,* someone who fakes enthusiasm for a company or product because he or she is getting paid to do so. After about 15 minutes of conversation with her, we're assured she's not an astroturfer.

Her online moniker is "Red Cart Romance." We'll call her RCR. She describes herself as an "Internet dork and Target lover, endcap whore, and $1 section addict." RCR says addicts like her "hide Target bags from their husbands, make up excuses to go to Target, and simply feel orgasmic by the thought." She writes about products at the store or *Target.com* that capture her imagination, especially products in the $1 section.

"I love the $1 section but lately I have been ho-hum about it," she writes in one blog post. "Right now I am just a giant HO about it as they have *Napoleon Dynamite* magnets!! Oh and pens, and pads and more magnets and pads and ugh it's the best. I am pretty much certain that he's my soul mate." A trivia game called Coffee Smarts that Target featured on its Web site snagged her attention. "I LOVE coffee. I drink coffee all day. Coffee is my crack. This is why I think that this little product is funny. I adore little games like this to play with my friends around the coffee table. Heh—coffee table, I am hysterical," she wrote. "I also love my *Desperate Housewives* tarot card game. It's funny to play it with your parents."

As a Fanatic, she's generous with praise and uncompromising with advice. "OK, [Target clothing designer] Isaac Mizrahi is amazing. Love him, but seriously he needs to get better at women's measurements. He needs to feel a woman's breast and take some measurements. Awful, awful. I wonder sometimes if there is a landfill of Isaac clothing out there filled to the brim of all of his great design ideas because no one could wear them? Sad."

When Target announced a new line of high-end designer wear sporting an embroidered red bull's-eye logo in 2006 to be sold only at a trendy Los Angeles boutique, RCR wrote: "Target is a Sell Out—they are sellin' out to the fads and the faddiest store ever." The *Washington Post* used that quote in a story about the new line, and she's been quoted frequently by other media outlets, too.

Her writing has amassed a sizable cart of fans; some 100,000 people visit her site a month, and she claims "over 1.5 million addicts comforted since June 2005." She thinks many readers are like her: young mothers who are value shoppers. Like other citizen marketers we spoke with, she is proficient in HTML and blogging tools. She spends about one or two hours per week posting and reading the site's e-mail. Based on her traffic numbers, RCR is confident her blog drives sales to *Target.com*. (She later removed the affiliate link; "too much of a hassle.") Maybe not enough traffic to change the world but enough to make a difference. "I have people emailing me all the time telling me that they have bought things that I talk about. They get off the computer and they run to the store. Or they buy it online," she tells us.

After the first call with John, the corporate marketing manager, Target seemed to embrace her. They exchanged e-mails for several months. He offered the services of their agency to help with any design needs for the blog. Perhaps, he wondered, if she could offer the company advice on how this blogging stuff worked. She hadn't started the blog to become a consultant for the company, so she said her reaction was one of surprise. Eventually, e-mails with John became sporadic and then died off. Other employees unofficially stay in touch; one wrote that Target CEO Robert Ulrich is a regular reader. She heard that Slave to Target was featured at a company conference attended by 5,000 employ-ees. Internally, the company seems to talk a lot *about* her. She wonders why the company doesn't ever talk *to* her. "It still boggles me why they don't talk to me. Why wouldn't they want to hear what their ultimate fan thinks?"

Her jovial mood soured. Employees now just e-mail tips about new products, and the company's PR firm blasts her with press kits about seasonal promotions. They think of her as a sales tool. Being considered a tool causes resentment. "I love what they carry but bottom line, they're still corporate America. I don't think they are ever going to change. They don't care really what I have to say. They'll have these really cool designs but they won't bow down to my level. They're afraid to know what their customers really want. They're really just a bunch of suits." Target wouldn't talk to us, either. "Target doesn't participate in interviews for books and would not comment on the blog you mentioned," a company spokeswoman told us.

The Slave to Target blogger illustrates the Power of One to accentuate affinity. Her focus on Target and Target only is a valida-tion point for the thousands of people who read her blog: they, too, can be fans of the retailer and feel giddy (or dismissive) about the company and some of its products. The size of her audience indi-cates a substantial interest in her work and, by extension, a validation of her relevance. Put into the context of a meme, her ability with the turn of a phrase has the potential to create an idea that leaps off the page and sticks in the minds of readers. (For example, we now know that if we ever meet Isaac Mizrahi, we are going to tell him that he needs to feel a woman's breast to become a better clothing designer.) As a Fanatic, she has a much greater chance of helping Target sell some of its more unique products to a plugged-in, early adopter audience of young mothers, surfing on their broadband connections and reading blogs, than those who are not online.

Let's return for a moment to the imitative function of memes. "All life evolves by the differential survival of replicating entities," Dawkins writes in *The Selfish Gene*. The gene replicates itself in all living beings to pass on the instructions of living. The next-generation gene survives because it does a great job of imitating its predecessor. Which leads us to Diet Coke and Mentos.

In the summer of 2006, thousands of online videos demonstrated how combining Diet Coke and the candy Mentos created a shooting geyser of soda. The most famous video of the summer featured two men in smocks who employed 101 two-liter bottles of Diet Coke and 523 Mentos candies to create a choreographed fountain of Diet Coke geysers. It was truly a spectacle video. Professional juggler Fritz Grobe and attorney Stephen Voltz, both of whom belong to a Maine theater company, created the video, and in less than two weeks, their video had been viewed more than 800,000 times on video-sharing site *Revver.com*. It would be easy to assume Grobe and Voltz had dreamed up the Diet Coke and Mentos idea themselves and the thousands of other videos were copycats.

But the Diet Coke and Mentos experiment had been spreading in the teacher community for years. It seems to have started with Steve Spangler, a Denver, Colorado, schoolteacher who launched a business to create science education teaching tools and specialty toys. A favorite science lesson was to teach kids the science of soda pop. He even wrote a book, called *Fizz Factor: 50 Amazing Experiments with Soda Pop,* which featured the Diet Coke and Mentos trick. He first demonstrated it on live television in March 2002 during a local television newscast. He followed that with an encore performance for the station in the summer of 2005. The video was archived on the station's Web site. It seems to be from that site that the meme began to spawn interest.

Grobe and Voltz say they were inspired for their video by seeing one of the online videos of the demonstration. "We wanted to make it bigger and better and turn it into something theatrical," said Grobe. As a meme, the Diet Coke and Mentos experiment had all of the instructions necessary to replicate it, and thousands of people did. It was not until the meme had a more efficient replicator—in this case, the online video-sharing sites—that it leapt into the creative minds of Grobe and Voltz, who elevated it to new levels of cultural awareness.

The reactions of Coke and Mentos to the surprising free marketing both received couldn't have been more different and pronounced.

Mentos: "We are tickled pink by it," a spokesman said. The company spends less than $20 million on advertising annually and estimates the value of online buzz to be "over $10 million."

Coke: "We would hope people want to drink [Diet Coke] more than try experiments with it," a spokeswoman said. She adds that the "craziness with Mentos . . . doesn't fit with the brand personality" of Diet Coke.

When anyone can be a content creator, publisher, broadcaster, or citizen marketer, there's bound to be more stuff to know, more stuff to entertain us. Thousands of Diet Coke and Mentos videos dot the video-sharing sites already. How many more do we need? Is it possible to make another interesting Diet Coke and Mentos video, and if so, how would we know about it? In the bigger meme picture, how do we separate the interesting stuff from the merely imitative? Digg's answer is social bookmarking, when its community members nominate interesting stuff for the benefit of the community. It is up to the community to determine what's interesting. But what if your own network is filled with hundreds of thousands or millions of items, and your community is less inclined to vote? How do you spot the interesting stuff in your own network? Or the important stuff? How do you make trend-spotting more *efficient?*

Create an "interestingness" algorithm. That's the idea of photo-sharing site Flickr. It has more than 200 million photos in its network, and it helps visitors find the interesting ones by examining the behavior of Flickr's visitors. It watches many of its members add a photo to their list of favorites, the number of visitors for each photo plus their comments, and less subtle data, like the relationship between the person who uploaded the photo and the people who are commenting. It does all of this in the background using a heavy-duty data-mining process to spit out a daily report of "interesting" photos among the hundreds of millions it hosts. The photos unearthed by the interestingness algorithm are usually striking photographs—beautifully composed and lit with interesting subjects in front of the camera lens.

"The act of consumption is itself becoming an act of production," said Yahoo's Bradley Horowitz during a chat we had with him at Yahoo's research center in Berkeley, California. (Yahoo is the parent company of Flickr.) "As I navigate through Flickr as a consumer, even if I never upload a photo or become an author per se, my very navigation is informing what we call 'interestingness.' The system is watching what I am doing, what I'm saving as a favorite, what I'm blogging about." Voting is a democratized way of determining interest and ranking while "interestingness" is something of an ethnographic scout, automatically aggregating the normal behavior of people and applying a mathematical formula against it. "Interestingness relies more on implicit measures, things that people were doing through their normal course of behavior through the system," Horowitz told us. "We simply leverage those to surface value back to other users."

CHAPTER SEVEN

How to Democratize Your Business

The future is already here.
It's just not very evenly distributed.

William Gibson

Creating a new product is betting that someone will purchase it. The same could be said for how a company determines its prices, inventory, manufacturing, and store-shelf requirements. Bets, bets, and more bets. For most companies, it's like studying card counting, then going to Vegas with $5 million and hoping for the best at the Mirage. Considering the 85 percent failure rate of new products, launching a new one is like betting against the house.

Two guys have rearranged that scenario and covered most of their bets. Their company asks thousands of its customers to design products, then vote on which ones they would buy. Once the votes are in, their company manufactures a finite number of the products the customers designed and voted on. If those sell out and customers want more, it's time to vote again. It is on-demand supply and demand. Without the benefit of complete educations or formal business training, these two guys, young guys really, have eliminated a good deal of the inherent, traditional risk of making products by involving customers deeply in the decision-making process. They make millions of dollars doing it. They've never had a flop. Talk about democratizing the business.

That's the essence of Threadless. Jake Nickell and Jacob DeHart have created a model of democratized participation that has propelled their T-shirt manufacturing business to become a $20 million company in five years. Customer-citizens create the T-shirt designs. Some are hobbyist designers; others are pros—there's no class distinction because it's an egalitarian playing field. Then on the company's Web site, *Threadless.com,* customers discuss the designs and vote for their favorites, indicating which ones they're inclined to buy. It's all done within the Threadless community, where all visitors can have their own blog and their own Threadless page. With several hundred thousand members, it's a good-sized city. It's a *politeia:* a business model of the future, determined by its citizen customers. It's not all without risk, though.

Nickell and DeHart work with a ticking time bomb. When they drive to their Chicago office in the Andersonville section of town, just blocks away from the Rosehill Cemetery, they turn on their computers to face the bomb.

"Our community could destroy us if they wanted to," Nickell says without a hint of irony. When we met Jake and Jacob—the two Jakes—one sunny day, Nickell was still recovering from the close call he'd just had with the community. He largely designs and codes the Web site himself. He loves to redesign it, too, and he often does. "When we started out, I think we were redesigning the site about every other week," he said. But the latest redesign went badly. He lost track of where he was and, in an instant, deleted all of the customers' blog posts. Just like that. He and others in the company scrambled to recover the posts from backup files. They launched recovery programs. They called their Web hosting company. It didn't look good, and Nickell was mortified.

When it was time to inform the community, Nickell posted an apology and explained the circumstances. The bomb didn't go off. It tried to solve Nickell's problem for him. Community members tried to dig up their posts from Google's cache system and repost them. One guy wrote a program to help the community transfer Google-cached posts back to Threadless. One user said maybe it was all for the better. "Sometimes it's good to have a clean slate," he wrote. Public relations disaster averted.

The Threadless community wields a tremendous amount of power, maybe more than we have seen with any company. Every day, thousands of them engage in spirited online discussions about T-shirts, designs, colors, what's cool, what isn't, and who the cool designers are. Then they vote on the 150 or so designs that are submitted to the community each day from around the world. Threadless will then manufacture several of them several weeks later. The community does this on a Web site that is part voting booth, coffeehouse, art gallery, and dorm. In other words, a social network. One of its key benefits is loyalty; 40 percent of the customers are repeat purchasers.

Nickell and DeHart, both college dropouts, met while they were members of an online art community called *Dreamless.org*. "We lived and breathed that community," Nickell said. (The genesis of "Threadless" is from the two Jakes having met on a "thread" on the Dreamless forum.) Their passion for the Dreamless community and the creativity it inspired led the two Jakes to an idea: "We wanted to give back to the [Dreamless] community, so we ran a competition to make products from people's art," Nickell explained. That competition evolved into the Threadless Web site, and it enabled them to host a competition every week.

Several years later, the company still holds a weekly design competition to determine what T-shirts it should manufacture and sell; with 150 designs submitted daily and about 8 percent of the community part of that process, the stakes are millions of dollars higher. That's where the democratization of forecasting demand comes in. Each shirt gets hundreds, sometimes thousands of votes on a 0–5 scale. Just above the 5 is a checkbox to indicate the voter's purchase intent: "I'd buy it." All of the data generated in this process is displayed on the site: each design entry shows the number of people who have rated it, the number of days left to vote on it, and the number of comments about it. Each week, about four to six winning designs are picked and printed as a limited edition of 1,200 shirts. Winning designers get $1,500 cash, $300 store credit, and a special-edition T-shirt every month for a year.

Inventory data is displayed in real time, too, democratizing the selection process as customers decide to buy a shirt that's nearly sold out or one whose inventory is still relatively plentiful. Data inventory provide clues on which shirts are more popular among men than women and which shirts are more popular with bigger customers than smaller ones. Each design sell outs within six months; 90 percent of all designs sell out within two months.

Just as municipalities worry about voter turnout, Threadless does, too, so it offers incentives to improve participation rates. Besides the design contest and the chance to win money and free shirts, every printed shirt has its own photo gallery. Community members are encouraged to upload a digital self-portrait that features a Threadless shirt. They're given a $1.50 credit for each photo and $15 if it's selected for the product page.

Except for a weekly e-mail newsletter, the company doesn't do much marketing. It relies on word of mouth and the work of its Street Team, an affiliate program, which pays a monetary reward for shirts purchased through an affiliate's Web site. Threadless even has fan Web sites. One of them, the Loves Threadless blog, participates in the marketing by generating buzz for new shirts.

We asked the two Jakes to describe the qualities that have driven the company's success. They'd already thought about this. "Allow your content to be created by the community. Put your project in their hands. Let your community grow itself, then reward them for making your project possible." Success has bred copycats. Similar online democratized T-shirt businesses have sprung up in France, Italy, Brazil, and England.

Applied to other industries and their business models, the Threadless model of a collaborative citizenry could make it possible for a company to create a more reliable forecasting system for choosy customers. It could more accurately gauge demand for trendy products. It could create a trustworthy source of repeat purchasers. It could help identify a lemon before it becomes an expensive lemon. They key, as the two Jakes illustrate, is to build a community with a stake in outcomes. That identifies a fundamental problem with most product research: it's often based on a representative sample of the imagined target audience that's cobbled together as a focus group. The group tests a product whose manufacturer may or may not be disclosed and might have little or no buy-in toward the outcome. They take their $50, go home, and move on with their lives. It's artificial reality. The Threadless community members invest themselves in the company by acting on their own interests *on behalf of the company.* A community eliminates the star-chamber effect—a small, secret group of decision makers with little or no sense of responsibility to a community since each follows his or her self-interests. The Threadless business model easily and efficiently tracks and quantifies the market-helping behaviors of its customers. It's a simple concept but a breakthrough achievement.

~

Throughout the book, we've talked about the "democratization" of technology, engagement, and decision-making. To democratize something is to make it more socially equitable or available to a broader array of interested people. The principles of democracy are designed to guard against power being concentrated in star chambers, monarchies, dictatorships, or centralized governments. Democracy distributes power and responsibility to the masses; in the case of republics, power is distributed to freely elected representatives. With the arrival of social media, affordable broadband, and less-expensive technologies, distributing power to communities of interest has never been easier or more important. With control slipping out of control, communities of interest are assuming power on their own and leading conversations about brands, products, companies, or organizations. By working with We, the *citizens,* companies are bound to reduce their risk of failure by embracing the principles of democracy and participating in established democratized forums or creating their own. They reduce risk by distributing it more evenly.

If the roots of citizenship have grown from the seeds of democracy, what is democracy? And what principles of democracy should a democratized forum follow?

Defining *democracy* is difficult, even for the U.S. State Department, whose job is to promote democracy to countries lacking it. "Although the term is ubiquitous in today's world, explaining 'democracy' can be challenging," the agency writes on its Web site, where "principles of democracy" handouts are shared via downloadable pamphlets. But it could be safely argued that freedom and liberty are the most precious principles of democracy. If liberty protects citizens from the arbitrary application of authority, then freedom is the guarantee of personal expression, whether it's standing on the street corner railing against the government or practicing any form of religion. For Americans, that guarantee is defined by the 45 words of the First Amendment:

> Congress shall make no law respecting an establishment of religion, or prohibiting the free exercise thereof; or abridging the freedom of speech, or of the press; or the right of the people to peaceably to assemble, and to petition the government for a redress of grievances.

By examining existing and popular democratized forums focused on products, brands, companies, or people, we see an underlying and fundamental principle: freedom of speech. Restrictions on speech that prohibit or limit criticism of a brand, company, or product may be good for the company, but they're onerous and pointless for a community. Anarchy isn't the rule, for there are existing legal protections against libel and slander. Guidelines on those important civil considerations should be clear and enforced. However, a democratized forum that restricts or eliminates criticism sacrifices its credibility. Even if that criticism is occasionally biting, rude, or painful. Other democratic principles include majority rule, decentralized power, free and fair elections, and the rule of law. Threadless has limited its risk by relying on a majority-rule system for determining most of its products (it may elect not to make T-shirts that prove to be too difficult or expensive to manufacture or violate copyright laws), and majority rule determines replenishing supply. How organizations adopt and interpret democratic principles for their communities is bound to be an ongoing discussion, one that's carried on with the community itself.

~

What inspires citizen marketers to create content on behalf of companies, brands, products, or people? Inspiration is, like lightning, hard to predict. Creating a sufficient brew of personal relevance that inspires citizen marketers or 1 Percenters is the job of leaders who have an intimate knowledge about their customers' motivations, desires, and habits. Nonetheless, social media have opened the floodgates of amateur culture to a wider and infinite aperture. With citizen marketers and 1 Percenters crashing the gates to create content about companies, brands, products, or people with or without official approval, this leaves companies with a variety of options to respond:

1. Say nothing publicly or privately to the people involved. (Apple's reaction to George Masters and the Neistat brothers.)

2. Make behind-the-scenes overtures but say nothing publicly. (Target's several interactions with the Slave to Target blogger but public "no comment" about her. We asked Modo & Modo to comment about Moleskinerie; at first the company said it would, then it decided not to.)

3. Provide terse recognition. (Coke's comments on people creating Diet Coke and Mentos geysers, Starbucks' acknowledgment of Winter the collector, Logitech's recognition of Bowiechick, and McDonalds' acknowledgment of McChronicles.)

4. Encourage company employees to participate. (The 44 TiVo employees who have registered with TiVoCommunity.)

5. Threaten or take legal action. (The film industry is notorious for suing people who build movie fan blogs and Web sites.)

6. Build programs or communities specifically for them.

7. Incorporate their ideas or work into your production system.

Items 6 and 7 prompt a question: what if a company discovers it has citizen marketers or wants to build a community of them? How to begin? Besides Threadless, several companies have been leading the way on democratizing engagement. The programs we've seen typically fall into what we call the "3 Cs" of working with citizen marketers: Contests, Co-creation, and Communities.

Contests

Contests are the quickest way to experiment with citizen-created content. We know from the 1% Rule that the total percentage of submissions to a contest as measured against the total number of potential participants will probably be low. When everyone is a publisher or broadcaster, competing for attention becomes a sizable challenge. With the right democratic principles in place, solid execution, and a respectful awareness about the potential of social media to spread word of mouth, a contest can improve fortunes and enhance loyalty. The more successful contests that solicit citizen-created media tend to involve brands or products with well-known histories and active fan communities. Let's look at several examples of company-sponsored contests designed to turn everyday people into citizen marketers.

1. Converse Gallery

The athletic shoe maker Converse invited its customers to submit 24-second films inspired by the decades-old Chuck Taylor brand. Everyone who entered the Converse Gallery contest would receive a pair of sneakers, and the grand prize winners would win $10,000 and have their work aired on MTV and other cable networks. The only rule was that submissions had to be "positive, original, and inspiring." Other than that, and providing royalty-free sound files if filmmakers needed soundtrack music, the level of interpretation was wide open. "Our customers tend to be creative, and we've given them the biggest canvas we have to express themselves—our advertising," said Converse's global marketing chief, Erick Soderstrom.

The company launched the contest in August 2004. Almost three months later, filmmakers had submitted 1,800 short films from 15 countries. A variety of entertaining and puzzling entries arrived, including "The Amazing Russell," which featured a man jumping a line of old Chuck Taylor sneakers on a vintage Schwinn girl's bicycle. (This film was later selected as a winner and was shown on several cable television networks.) Within a month of the gallery's launch, traffic to the Converse Web site surged 66 percent. Shoe sales on the Converse Web site doubled, and overall company sales increased 12 percent in the quarter compared to the previous quarter.

The Converse Gallery exemplified the numerous benefits of soliciting citizen-created content. It was a well-designed, well-executed contest with a sweet grand prize. The theme of the contest was broad, and that may not work for every organization. It worked for Converse because it has a rich history. Converse first began to manufacture its All Star sneaker in 1917. They were officially baptized as Chuck Taylor All Stars in 1923 when Converse formally recognized the evangelism work of amateur basketball player Chuck Taylor. He wasn't the most notable basketball player on the court, but off the court, he had great game. He was an inexhaustible advocate for basketball and Converse, so the company hired him as a full-time spokesman. Taylor spent 35 years working for Converse on a nonstop "Evangelist Tour" (the tour's actual name), spreading the word about basketball and Converse around the world. Chuck Taylor, the person, was the message. That developed the cultural platform for Converse, and the Chuck Taylor All Stars have been called the "official shoe of the counter-culture." Rebels in the 1950s wore black Chucks with white T-shirts and black leather jackets. Hippies wore multicolored Chucks in the 1960s, and legions of punk rockers wore them in the 1980s. That has translated into more than 750 million pairs of Chuck Taylor All Star shoes sold in 144 countries. Creators for the Converse Gallery had a rich and varied cultural history to work with.

2. Ban This!

While talking with a group of teens one day in 2005, the makers of Ban deodorant learned that their marketing wasn't very interesting. "Outstanding odor and wetness protection" didn't resonate with teenage girls. Furthermore, the company was marketing *at* them, the girls said. "Why not give us some say on what can and should be said?"

That inspired Ban to wonder what girls and women aged 12 to 20 would wish to ban in their lives. A "Ban _____" contest invited Web site visitors to select a photograph, or upload their own, and fill in the blank. From the submissions, the company would select nine semifinalists, and visitors would vote for a favorite. Semifinalists were awarded $1,500, and the grand prize winner won a day with the actress Hilarie Burton. The company launched the contest September 2005; three months later, it had 4,000 submissions. When the "ads" of the nine semifinalists were featured on the Ban Web site, traffic shot up 150 percent, more than any other advertising effort it had undertaken. After a three-year decline, sales of Ban rose 13.6 percent in the 52 weeks ending November 27, 2005.

By asking teenage girls what they would "ban," the company exposed a natural vein of frustrations related to puberty, school, parents, boys, and social pressures. It was an ideal contest theme. But Ban did not have an established community of young female fans, primarily because it was regarded as "your mother's deodorant." After updating the product's packaging design, they launched the contest and advertised it through ads in teen magazines, but inevitably, word spread via instant messaging, e-mail, and blogs.

Had the contest makers allowed the community to establish the semifinalists, we surmise that all numbers related to the program would have risen. Contest entrants would have encouraged friends in their networks to vote for their slogan. There was no opportunity to comment on any slogan and no way to link to individual slogans. Although the contest Web site lives on, it's in a different format and does not display the history of the slogans, the semifinalists, or the winner. It's moved on to a new contest.

3. Spread Firefox

Firefox is the free Web browser that was developed and is maintained by a group of volunteer programmers from around the world. The nonprofit organization behind the browser, the Mozilla Foundation, launched a campaign in December 2005 to promote the browser's latest version. It encouraged fans with webcams to record a brief testimonial for the browser or, if they were inclined, to create a more elaborate 30-second ad for the browser. Mozilla employees picked the webcam testimonial winners. A panel of judges from advertising agencies, Hollywood, and television would determine the 30-second ad winners. The testimonial winner would receive a $500 *Amazon.com* gift certificate. Winners of the

30-second ad contest received higher-end prizes, such as a $5,000 gift certificate and some electronics goodies.

Mozilla received 600 webcam testimonials from 41 different countries. For the ad contest, it received 280 submissions. Downloads of the browser went from 100 million in October 2005 to 200 million by July 2006. Webcam testimonial submissions included a lyrical, singer-songwriter ode: "Firefox, I like to use you on my box. Oh, Firefox, you really rock." Submissions to the 30-second contest included a rap-influenced number: "Made by Mozilla, it's the pop-up killa. All the other browsers are just plain vanilla." The nonprofit entity behind Firefox had been building a democratized community of fans since the browser's introduction in November 2004. They called the community "Spread Firefox," and by the end of 2005, it had grown to 100,000 registered members. It was largely comprised of young, tech-savvy men who worked collaboratively to market the browser to the world. The Spread Firefox community was so fervent that it raised $250,000 to feature Firefox in a two-page ad in the *New York Times*. Firefox had a built-in community to which it could communicate easily and solicit contest submissions. What worked against the contest was the custom technology it used for submissions. Testimonial contributors were required to use the technology to create and submit their work, and of the 600 submitted, only 320 were usable. Asa Dotzler, who worked on the campaign for Mozilla, said the customized Web application they created was too complicated and caused contributors sound-recording problems. Nonetheless, Mozilla says it was happy with the results.

4. "The Rock"

In April 2006, Kansas City radio station 98.9 FM, "The Rock," asked listeners to create and submit a TV commercial on behalf of the radio station. Listeners submitted 360 entries that featured all manner of babies, grandmas, and mullets. The commercials weren't pretty, but that was the point. Although the station encouraged listeners to vote for their favorites, it ultimately decided the winner: an ad that featured two contestants who compete in a variety of sporting events with bags over their heads. The first bag read "98.9 the Rock." The second: "Other Radio Stations." As you might guess, the Other Radio Stations guy loses each event. The station awarded the three teenage filmmakers a $20,000 grand prize. The contest generated a good deal of interest and press attention in Kansas City.

After the grand prize was awarded, the station removed all of the video entries from its Web site. The hundreds of inbound links to the contest and the videos are dead. That's unfortunate, because citizen-created content can generate buzz indefinitely. The work of listeners could be considered a totem of their loyalty and creativity, but the station has inexplicably removed the totems. If the experience of The Rock teaches us anything, it's keep citizen-created content online. Storage is cheap, and Google has a long memory.

5. Wal-Mart

Back-to-school time is important for retailers, especially the biggest of them all: Wal-Mart. To promote its back-to-school clothes to teenagers, the company launched the Wal-Mart "School Your Way" contest in July 2006. It was a pseudosocial networking site like MySpace, but it was restricted to teens ages 13 to 18. They were encouraged to create a video or personalized page "to discuss, illustrate, express their individuality [and] how it is reflected in their personal style, taste in fashions/accessories, interests, activities, etc., and to consider how Wal-Mart helps support their personal style and self-expression through the depth and breadth of products Wal-Mart offers." The grand prize was being featured in a Wal-Mart TV commercial or receiving Sony electronics or a trip for two to Los Angeles. Wal-Mart preloaded the site with three personal pages and three videos that were scripted and professionally produced.

The contest launched in July 2006 and was closed to entries less than a month later. The contest rules were 6,000 words long, or about 12 printed pages. During the contest period, 677 personal areas were created and approximately 5 videos were created. (The site did not provide a way to see all produced videos, so the number is an approximation based on viewing 130 random pages.) The one user-created video we found would not play. "School Your Way" was Wal-Mart's first attempt at creating community, but the company made the window of participation small and restrictive. Wal-Mart is a controversial company, and its "low prices" stance has forever been its trademark; the lack of aspiration surrounding Wal-Mart is a challenge for the company's marketers.

As a poor knockoff of MySpace, "School Your Way" failed because the contest period was too short and the imprisoning limitations of the site's design prevented any sociability. No linking was allowed. It was virtually impossible to find members. The scripted language and overall nature of the site's prepopulated kids were inauthentic. *Advertising Age* said that the site "proves just how painfully uncool it is to try to be cool." Two kids the magazine interviewed did not give the site high marks. "Some of the kids looked like they were trying to be supercool, but they weren't at all, and they were just being kind of weird," said Amy Kandel, 14, of Columbus, Ohio. Pete Hughes, 18, wasn't impressed either: "Are these real kids? It just seemed kind of corny to me." Research groups reported they received increasingly bad feedback from teenage girls about Wal-Mart in contrast to Target, especially about Wal-Mart's apparent lack of store cleanliness, messy layout, and lack of stylish attire. Given this information, are we surprised there was a lack of interest in the contest?

Co-creation

When a company "co-creates," it involves customers in a partnership to produce a product or service. The more it involves customers in the production process, the more they will take an ownership stake in the success of the product and the company. Co-creation can be simple—like personalizing a product label, as small-but-popular Jones Soda in Seattle and Blowfly Beer in Australia do—to complex—like having customers design the product, as Threadless does. Let's look at few examples of companies that have co-created products with the citizen marketers.

1. "Hips Don't Lie"

Spend 30 minutes scrolling through the various amateur videos on YouTube, and one thing you'll notice is that people love to create their own music videos, preferably in front of a webcam lip-synching a favorite hit song or dancing to it. YouTube is rife with imitation-as-flattery. How else to explain the rather obvious yet brilliant idea of Epic Records to ask fans of Columbian-born singer Shakira to submit short, booty-shaking video clips of themselves to be included on a fan-only music video for the song "Hips Don't Lie"? That's what Epic did in 2006, and about 10,000 fans took up the offer. After culling the submissions, the record company created a mashup video that zoomed to the number-one spot on Yahoo Music. The fan video was viewed more than a million times in the first few weeks of its release.

That's one part of the story. The other part is that when Shakira's album, *Oral Fixation Vol. 2* was released in November 2005, it stalled. "Hips Don't Lie" wasn't part of the original release, so Epic released it again in March 2006 with "Hips Don't Lie." Listeners loved the song. The fan-based video certainly fanned the flames of interest in the album. After its rerelease, *Oral Fixation Vol. 2* sold a million copies in the United States and was certified gold in 14 countries (the number of sales to reach gold status varies by country). "Hips Don't Lie" was the number-one downloaded song on iTunes for several weeks in 2006 and hit number one on the *Billboard* Hot 100. It eventually became the most-played pop song in American radio history: 9,637 times in a week. It is one of the few songs in history to reach number one in almost every charting country in the world.

Is there a correlation between the fan video mashup and the album's success? A hit song is a hit song, but creating a fan-only video (there was another that only featured Shakira herself) was a natural reflection of what was already happening in the citizen-content culture. Epic provided fans with another forum for what many of them were already doing, and it turned out to be a grassroots favorite.

2. "Awesome!"

The Beastie Boys have a history of mixing things up since they first started rapping to their unique, punk-rock funk in 1979, including posting a cappella tracks of the band's songs to their Web site and encouraging fans to sample them for their own mashups. When the band wanted to commemorate its October 2004 sold-out concert at Madison Square Garden, they mixed it up again. The Beasties asked fans to film the show so they could use the footage to create a concert movie.

The band gave 50 fans video cameras and instructed them to shoot whatever they wanted, as long as they did it with passion. It took editors a full year to comb through 100 hours of material, including lip-synching fans, beer runs, and trips to the bathroom. They called the film *"Awesome: I Fuckin' Shot That"* (yes, that is the actual name), and it debuted at the 2006 Sundance Film Festival to mostly positive reviews. The BBC called it "immediate, intoxicating, and nearly as good as being there yourself." "What I really like about the movie is that the people shot it," said Adam Yauch, band member and director of the film. "That's the essence of hip-hop or punk. It's not like 'these people made it.' We all made it together."

3. The Vespa Way

Piaggio Group is the Italian manufacturer of Vespa scooters. From its research, it knew that 65 percent of prospective motor scooter buyers visit the Vespa USA Web site. But they also found that 56 percent of their prospects visited other sites to see what people were saying about the scooters. With a solid understanding about the influence existing Vespa owners could wield, Piaggio asked two of its customer evangelists to blog about their experiences as Vespa owners. It launched and sponsored the Vespaway blog, an alternative to a corporate blog, but the bloggers do the work for free. They are free to post whatever they choose, and their compensation is free Vespa merchandise and invitations to company events. Blog posts from the customers discuss Vespa mileage, a trip report from a national Vespa show, and how to turn the plastic red panels on the back of the Vespa into working reflectors.

Piaggio sees the Vespaway blog as an extension of traditional scooter clubs, in which enthusiasts of the vehicles gather to discuss issues and ideas, says Paolo Timoni, chief executive of Piaggio USA. "This new blog is the way to do it nowadays," he said.

4. Lego's Mindstorm

Denmark-based Lego is a giant in little plastic toy bricks for kids, but its Mindstorms product has fans of all ages. Lego Mindstorms combines programmable bricks with electric motors, sensors, plastic bricks, and other Lego pieces to build robots. The company searched online Lego user groups and Web sites and tapped four expert customers to help it design the next-generation product from the ground up. For 11 months, the four customers virtually worked along side Lego engineers, exchanging plenty of e-mails filled with ideas for new sensors, redesigning input ports, and stabilizing firmware. The customers' payment for all of this work? A few Lego crane sets and Mindstorms prototypes. The customers even paid their own airfares to Lego headquarters in Denmark. "Pretty much the comment from all four of us was 'They're going to talk to us about Legos, and they're going to pay us with Legos?'" said Steve Hassenplug, one of the customers from Lafayette, Indiana. "'They actually want our opinion?' It doesn't get much better than that."

Community

Companies that create their own communities are democratizing their call centers. They distribute knowledge to a greater number of people. They take what has typically been a highly structured and systematized resolution system and break it open for the masses to hack. If a company is lucky, the community will hack it enthusiastically and build it into a very vertical Wikipedia of knowledge. If that happens, then a company has created two real tangible assets: an expanded knowledge base and an identifiable database of citizen-owners.

Academics who study online communities say their dynamics are no different than established, real-world communities. Sociologists say there are three core components to understanding the dynamics of community:

1. Consciousness of kind. It's that intrinsic sense of being "a New Yorker" and not like people in Los Angeles or Lisbon. When the two Jakes met on Dreamless, it was a natural partnership because the community's consciousness of kind was well developed.

2. Shared rituals and traditions. New York is rich with tradition, like the Macy's Thanksgiving Day Parade and the New York Marathon. Those are two spectacle events, but New York's boroughs are rich with their traditions, parades, and parties, too. At Threadless, the two Jakes release a new batch of community-created T-shirts every week.

3. A sense of moral responsibility to the community. By reading hundreds of comments on the designs of T-shirts at Threadless, we found a community that supports the work of its designers. Critiques of designs are direct but usually not intentionally hurtful. By contrast, the rough-and-tumble Digg community may taunt, ridicule, and slap. A bit like pro wrestling. It's not for everyone, but the Threadless community isn't for everyone, either.

Here's how other companies have democratized their communities, what spurred the development, and the early results they've been able to achieve.

1. Discovery Education

For about ten years, videocassettes and VCRs ruled the world. VCRs were in about 90 percent of all American homes, and Blockbuster stores did blockbuster business with videotape rentals. The rise of the videocassette had a big effect on schools, too, as VCRs replaced unreliable films and filmstrips.

The glory years of VCRs were often bureaucratic ones for teachers. If a teacher wanted to commemorate Veterans' Day by showing a video of the 1941 surprise attack on Pearl Harbor, she might have to fill out a form requesting a tape and file it with the school's (or school district's) "media center" several days to several weeks in advance. A media center worker would search for the tape among thousands of titles and load it and dozens of other tapes into a van for a driver to ferry them across town to the school. That's a lot of labor for one tape.

By early 2001, more than 90 percent of all American K–12 schools had Internet access. Now, hundreds of thousands of American teachers can download digital videos clips directly from companies like Discovery Education in minutes and drag them into a PowerPoint file.

Discovery Education owns a good chunk of this market. (It's a division of Discovery Communications, which owns the cable offerings Discovery Channel, Animal Planet, and the Travel Channel, among others.) It serves about 70,000 schools in the United States with a video-on-demand product called unitedstreaming. If a sixth-grade history teacher wants to teach a lesson about Pearl Harbor, she can choose from 178 video clips, 25 photos, 45 articles, and 2 quizzes from unitedstreaming's database and use as many of them as she wants, whenever she wants.

While Discovery owned a commanding lead of the market, it struggled with a nagging problem: usage levels of unitedstreaming in some school districts were lower than expected. Usage is a key metric. Districts have little interest in paying for something that's not widely used. Although some teachers were still getting comfortable using PCs, Discovery's research found that many teachers didn't know that unitedstreaming was already available at their school. Coni Rechner had been with the company since the product's inception and noticed how some teachers hosted their own unitedstreaming workshops at conferences, or explained the product's benefits to school district administrators, or demonstrated it for parents. They were evangelists and citizen marketers for the product.

That got Rechner thinking: build a program around the evangelism of teachers. She called it the Discovery Educator Network, and it unites educators who believe in digital media as a teaching tool. The DEN gives unitedstreaming's citizen marketers the tools to help them train other educators about instructional technologies, not just the product. "My goal was to build a list of these evangelists," Rechner recalled. "I wanted to figure out how we could support them with tools and also get their input for growing the product."

To build the program, Rechner hired 30 educators from around the United States who were existing evangelists for unitedstreaming. The 30 educators left their teaching jobs to become full-time employees of Discovery. Their mission is to spread the word about the DEN and recruit teachers to join the network. Like Chuck Taylor, they weren't hired as representatives to fulfill sales goals but as community builders. The community would be collected under an umbrella Web site armed with an array of social media. Teachers who join the network are encouraged to contribute content to it, such as their own PowerPoint files they use in the classroom. Educators seem to be inspired by the community's sharing. "I have made friends with other educators who share, no strings attached, because they believe [in] reaching all students and that all students should experience the best education has to offer," said Susan Little, a third-grade teacher at Palmetto Elementary in Fontana, California. Other tools like a discussion forum and events calendar provide a structure for the unstructured unitedstreaming trainings that Rechner had observed earlier. DEN members share their ideas and experiences on DEN-provided blogs. Nearly all of the content is created and synthesized by the community.

A year after the DEN had launched, unitedstreaming usage had increased 114 percent, and teachers who were DEN members used the product twice as much as non-DEN teachers. The usage rates at schools with a DEN member were 2.5 times higher than schools without one. More than 130,000 educators had participated in teacher-delivered face-to-face training events. Teachers had uploaded nearly 2,000 of their own teaching resources to share with other teachers. Finally, renewals of unitedstreaming jumped from 82 percent to 99 percent.

The DEN represented a number of firsts for Discovery Communications. The first division to have a blog. The first division to have an online democratized forum. The first division to hire an online community manager. Discovery Education's president, Steve Sidel, envisions the community model working its way across other parts of the corporation. He imagines that Discovery stores could be places for DEN members to gather for a lecture and coffee. Teachers could provide content for network shows, especially the Discovery Channel and the Learning Channel. "For Discovery Education, I do see the DEN being a critical part of our strategy in everything we do, from kindergarten–12 to pre-kindergarten, post-secondary, continuing education, recreational learning, the U.S., and around the world. And that is a big deal."

As the executive responsible for the DEN, Sidel is responsible for the charting the unexplored waters of community building for Discovery. Because his division sells content to dozens of countries beyond the United States, he has begun to think, for example, about the future of teachers in Indiana collaborating with teachers in India. "For the DEN to *not* become an international enterprise, that would be strange," he told us. "It *will* be an international enterprise. For the DEN to be artificially limited to some set number of teachers would be strange. And it won't be artificially limited. To the extent you can create engaging communities and the result of that community is that they that deliver things in the world that make the world a better place, I vote more not less community members."

2. QuickBooks Community

One day while listening in on phone calls to Intuit's customer-support center, Scott K. Wilder realized his company's call-center staff could never keep up with the variety and types of questions being asked by customers in so many specialized industries. If QuickBooks, the company's accounting software product, was going to develop intricate knowledge of its customers' varied businesses, then Intuit would need a forum for customers to share their knowledge online. Better knowledge would enable better support.

With the help of a contractor, Wilder launched QuickBooks Community in 2005 as a low-profile project. It was a forum for the 3.4 million users of QuickBooks—from the novice to the expert accountant—to share and exchange ideas, ask questions, and provide peer support.

Wilder divided the community into 61 different forums categorized by industry type (such as law firms, restaurants), tasks (such as inventory, payroll), products (such as enterprise solutions, online edition), country, and business issues. People who used to staff the call center now moderate the forums. QuickBooks employees maintain a series of blogs, including one that collects and organizes feedback from the community for the product-development group. After a year, the QuickBooks Community had 70,000 registered members and was hosting 100,000 visitors per month. Hundreds of significant changes to the QuickBooks products were made based directly on the feedback of the community. The changes are detailed on the Web site in a section called "Better Because of You."

3. Channel 9

When your company is routinely called "The Evil Empire" and your company founder is referred to as the "Gates from Hell," how do you soften the perception?

Microsoft's idea was to create a Web-based community. In 2004 it launched Channel 9, at *channel9.msdn.com.* Named after the in-flight channel on United Airlines that allows passengers to listen to what pilots in the cockpit are saying, Channel 9 exists outside of the company's product and marketing and public-relations groups. It's run by what the company calls its "platform evangelism" group, and Channel 9 is Microsoft's effort to let the many thousands of independent developers who rely on Microsoft technologies to create their own software products into the company cockpit. It's the anti-empire approach.

Access includes hundreds of video interviews that the Channel 9 team members have conducted with Microsoft developers, product managers, and executives about the company and its products. The video interviews exude and even rely on a decided amateurism. Camera work is shaky, lighting is uneven, and interviews are often more discussion than interview. The more popular videos demonstrate future versions of products like FoxPro and components of the Office suite. One of the most-viewed videos features CEO Steve Ballmer on why he loves "developers, developers, developers." Other segments of Channel 9 have evolved into a forum for developers to talk about software news and ideas. An attached wiki, a Web site that easily allows people to modify it, aggregates feedback and facilitates collaboration.

After two years online, Channel 9 had attracted 36,000 developers who became official members. Those developers had created more than 200,000 pieces of content while Microsoft employees had created 1,325 content items, consisting of videos, podcasts and screencasts. Channel 9 attracts a lot of spectators; by July 2006, it was hosting 4.5 million visitors per month.

Jeff Sandquist is one of Channel 9's founders. He says calling the site a "community" doesn't adequately explain its mission. "I like to think of the end goal for sites like Channel 9 is to have something that resembles a music festival. If you attend a music festival like Bumbershoot or Farm Aid, what you notice right away is that often the most interesting aspects of the event aren't always happening on the main stage. The people who are attending and the things they do often are more interesting than the performers on stage. With Channel 9 this is what we aspire to create. We dream of a day where the participation by our members either rivals or outshines the content that's happening on the main stage."

What Threadless established from its first day as a company, and what Microsoft, Intuit, and Discovery are working toward, is establishing *community as a core competency.* A 1990 article in the *Harvard Business Review* first proposed the idea of a core competency as "an area of specialized expertise that is the result of harmonizing complex streams of technology and work activity." Authors Gary Hamel and C. K. Prahalad called it the fundamental three or four things a company does exceptionally better than its competitors. Harmonizing complex streams of technology and activity easily describes the underpinnings of a community that is both creating and consuming content. Community is a core competency for Harley-Davidson. About 600,000 of its customers are members of the Harley Owners Groups (or HOGS, as they like to say). Members are scattered across 1,200 clubs in 100 countries, and they get together regularly for communal rides. Harley supports the group with how-to information and community facilitation.

Developing community as a core competency does not mean a company has to begin with programs like those of Harley-Davidson, Microsoft, Intuit, or Discovery. Creating a democratized forum can begin simply with a blog, as Dell did after noisy customers demanded the company establish a dialogue with them. A blog provides up-front and immediate qualitative feedback. It's a meme catcher.

The growth, popularity, and cultural influence of social networks YouTube and MySpace have underscored the strategic potential of community being a core competency. A network is as only strong as its members, and members are reluctant to help a clueless network organizer. CEOs must define core competencies and hold their organizations (and themselves) accountable for their success. As we have seen with Discovery, Intuit, and Microsoft, developing community as a core competency inside established companies can be and perhaps should be the domain of a skunk works project but done with the full blessing and support of the CEO.

~

That movies get made at all is something of a miracle.

Samuel L. Jackson, a reliably bankable actor, agreed to star in a movie called *Snakes on a Plane*. He loved the title, but, ironically, the studio couldn't find many other actors interested in the script because of the title. David R. Ellis eventually directed the film, but he'd been put off by the title, too. "Part of me said, 'That is a genius title,' and another part said 'You have got to be kidding.'" Even movie critic Roger Ebert publicly scoffed at the title: "How about this for another title: *Hand Down the Garbage Disposal.*"

So the studio changed it to *Pacific Air Flight 121*. That set off Jackson. "I knew I was going to do the movie when I saw the title," said Jackson, who plays an FBI agent protecting a witness against the Mob during a transcontinental flight. Of course, things go terribly wrong when the Mob tries to rub out the witness by way of poisonous snakes. "I think I have an audience member's sensibility, and the title just puts it all right out there. You either get it, or you don't. [New Line] wanted to call it *Pacific Air 121*. I told them that was the stupidest damn thing I ever heard." They changed the title back to *Snakes on a Plane*.

Filming for the August 18, 2006, release wrapped in the summer of 2005. But by the end of the year, buzz about *Snakes on a Plane* started to spread. Their imaginations fueled by a story line with a perfect meme—snakes on a plane—movie fans became citizen marketers. They started creating film trailers, movie posters, blogs, T-shirts, poems, and songs. One song's lyrics wondered what much of Hollywood had wondered: "There has got to be much more to it / This can't be a movie; no, it's too damn stupid / Snakes on a plane!" It became so common fans gave it an idiomatic handle: SoaP.

On Flickr, fans posted hundreds of photos of imaginary scenes and riffs of the title. There, "Snakes on a BBQ" and "Snakes on a Pug" were a few of the favorites. A few months later, Technorati turned up more than 21,000 blog posts about the movie, while Google found about 6 million citations. Soon it became an idiom among some people for "C'est la vie" or "Stuff happens." At *CafePress.com*, where anyone can create and sell apparel and other merchandise, fans created several hundred SoaP T-shirts; with the various combinations possible on CafePress, fans created more than 6,000 SoaP products in all. Fans created their own movie trailers and posted them to YouTube. Several look like real trailers, including the obligatory "The following PREVIEW has been approved for ALL AUDIENCES" screen and the New Line Cinema logo. They borrowed footage from airplane films and scenes of Jackson in other movies to create their own SoaP story lines.

Brian Finkelstein was in the middle of the fan frenzy. A 26-year-old Georgetown University Law School student by day, he spent a few hours each night categorizing and documenting all of the amateur content creation. (Finkelstein was the documentarian of the sleeping Comcast technician we mentioned in chapter 6.) On a whim, he launched Snakes on a Blog. His first post:

> Some of you know each other, others may not, but I'm calling all of your powers together because I have a goal that I cannot achieve alone. It's a goal of such lofty proportions that the mere thought of achieving it has me trembling in my darkened apartment. It's keeping me up at night. My goal, my quest, is to be an invited guest to the world premiere of the movie that is destined to change the world. A movie of such scope and awe that you need only read the title to understand everything you'll ever need to know about the

movie. The fact that it's staring Samuel L. Jackson is a mere afterthought to the magical title. I want to attend the glitzy Hollywood premiere of: *Snakes on a Plane.*

Almost immediately, fans started e-mailing Finkelstein their creative works, which he dutifully published. People sent SoaP stick-figure animations, poems, original songs, movie trailers, even a SoaP-inspired Sudoku puzzle. His attention to detail, including reports rich with data on how many people were involved with his site, stewed the juices of interest. Soon he was hosting 10,000 visitors every day, and it became the movie's de facto Web site. Finkelstein's small apartment in Washington, D.C., filled up quickly with fan-created art. New Line sent him a giant box of SoaP posters, most of which he gave away to blog readers.

We met Finkelstein in his apartment near the Georgetown section of D.C. He grew up in Westchester County, New York, and graduated from Tufts University before enrolling at Georgetown University. His only movie experience, besides attending them, was doing Web site design for a few theaters in Boston. We weren't the first people to ask him about his work; three television crews had been by in the past several weeks.

"Everyone who has had the experience of hearing the title and becoming enamored with it has wanted to find a way to be involved," he said. "Some people make T-shirts, some people make songs, and some people draw posters." Seven months after its launch, the blog had attracted a total of 915,000 visitors, who accounted for 3 million page views. His site had served 1.29 terabytes of data fulfilling 47 million requests for photos, icons, songs, and movie files he'd uploaded. He had posted 365 stories (about two per day). More than 4,288 comments had been posted, and 8,360 other blogs and Web site linked to his.

Why did Finkelstein volunteer to become a cataloger of the movie buzz? "It seemed like it would be fun. I would definitely call it a hobby." Is he surprised by all the attention that the blog had gotten? "Every cultural event or phenomenon that happens online has a focal point. It doesn't necessarily have to be something that started out planning to be the focal point. It just has to be something that people coalesce around. So in that respect it's not surprising. But in the fact that it happened to me is a little bit surprising. There's no reason that I should be the focal point. But, so be it."

We asked him how New Line responded to his work: "They called fairly early on to say that they were aware of what was happening online. They endorsed it and were excited about it. But they wanted to stay hands off because they knew that as soon as they got involved, or showed a heavy hand in controlling what was happening, people would not be interested in the movie anymore. [Basically] they said 'Hello, how ya doing? We are not going to sue you. Keep doing it. But you are on your own.'"

Working on the SoaP blog has been an education for Finkelstein the law student. "I've learned that that there is a surprising amount of talent and energy about things that people are not involved with if you give them a chance. I made a web page; it's not that much. But people are making songs and videos and putting a lot more time into this than I probably did. I find that surprising." He jokes that he's also learned that "occasionally movie studios won't sue people when they are appropriating their images. Copyright infringement doesn't always have to be a bad thing."

It doesn't have to be, but some media merchants are unconvinced. Finkelstein cites legal threats against fans of Harry Potter, Star Wars, and all manner of musical groups. "I would argue it's a mistake to go after your fans," he says. "The fan base is the people who are handing you money. I'd like to see that attitude change where [the fans] are the enemy."

Die-hard fans of the Star Wars and Star Trek franchises have been creating their own derivatives of those shows for years, thereby extending their mythology and affiliation. The SoaP phenomenon illustrates the potential of fan-created content *before* the release of a movie or product. New Line had yet to begin marketing the movie when fans involved themselves. New Line largely declined to talk to the press about the fans' work. The studio realized if it got involved in the publicity, "the organic, spontaneous feel [would] be gone," Finkelstein said. It was the work of fans and Finkelstein's blog that propelled the story into the arms of traditional one-way media outlets. Without anyone from New Line to talk about the film, media outlets from most of the major newspapers, networks, and the Associated Press turned to Finkelstein. "I've learned to give television interviews," he says.

What set SoaP apart from other films was the early feedback from self-selected, highly interested film fans. Ellis and New Line Cinema heard about it and took notice. Fans were expecting violence, graphic snakebites, and plenty of profanity from Jackson. One fan-created line was repeated endlessly by other fans: "I have had it with these motherfucking snakes on this motherfucking plane!" The line wound up on fan-created T-shirts and fan art. Jon Stewart, on Comedy Central's *The Daily Show,* used it repeatedly after seeing it on the Internet.

One problem was that the film had already finished principal photography. It was rated PG-13. "They restricted my cursing and they restricted the gore," said Jackson. "It was kind of a waste of time." So in early 2006, the filmmakers reshot parts of the movie to incorporate the fans' ideas. "We were fortunate," says Ellis. "We had the ability to listen to the audience before we finished, so we could totally deliver exactly what they dreamed of seeing." They upped the snake count and the death count. They added more nudity and, to the gratification of Jackson fans, more swearing, including the exact expletive-filled line fans loved. As Jackson told *TIME* magazine, "It's kind of difficult to watch me in a movie and not hear me say mother------ once."

Seeing fans take ownership of the film a year before its release convinced Ellis their input was valid. When he reshot parts of the movie to incorporate their work, that galvanized the fans but ignited a debate about the role of art and citizen collaboration. In a column for *Esquire* magazine, the pop-culture and music writer Chuck Klosterman said collaborating with fans makes SoaP "the Wikipedia version of a movie."

"If *Snakes on a Plane* is a commercial success . . . this brand of participatory, choose-your-own-adventure filmmaking is going to become a model. And that model will be terrible." Terrible, he submits, because it would tempt filmmakers to treat bloggers as a focus group, rendering movies idiotic and impersonal. He argues that artistic decisions by consensus don't work any better than giving one person complete autonomy. So why do it?

To reduce risk. Films, and to a larger degree, multimillion dollar projects, rely on multiple levels of collaboration to succeed. A film's principals collaborate because there is no formula for creating a good movie. If so, every movie would be good, if not great. "I have no ego," Ellis said, in a moment of confession, identifying what may really be the threat to people who argue that a community cannot be artistic. "You have to be smart enough to collaborate with everybody when you're making a movie, so why not work with the people you're making the movie for?"

John Heffernan is the film's screenwriter, and he says collaborating with fans improves the Hollywood process. "No one person ever makes a movie all by themselves," he said. "You're collaborating with development executives, you're collaborating with studio executives, you're collaborating with actors, the crew, your editors. Everybody has something to say. So if you're going to be listening to these people, you better be listening to the people who are going to put down $10 and watch the movie." As a screenwriter and, by extension, artist, Heffernan said he isn't threatened by altering a script based on fan feedback. "You'd be a fool not to give the audience what they want," he said. "You're not making this movie for yourself to watch in a private screening room. You're making it for people who you hope are going to like this movie and enjoy your vision."

What SoaP may have demonstrated is that big projects with multiple levels of collaboration can have multiple ownership levels inside and outside the corporate entity. "Personally, I think it's great," says Jackson. "[The fans] saved the movie."

As for Finkelstein, New Line finally invited him to the Hollywood premiere of the movie. His months of work as a citizen marketer fulfilled his dream. *Snakes on a Plane* was the number-one movie during its debut weekend, earning $15.3 million. In what can only be described as a buzz backlash, some traditional media called the opening weekend a disappointment. The *New York Times* said $15.3 million was a "letdown." "The tepid opening dashed the hopes of Hollywood," the *Times* wrote. Certainly, what's measured for success in the movie industry (but hardly anywhere else) is opening weekend box office figures. Never mind that the number one movie of the Sept. 8–10, 2006, weekend was *The Covenant,* which earned $8.8 million, followed by the heavily promoted Ben Affleck film *Hollywoodland,* which earned $5.9 million. (SoaP did earn $33 million after four weeks; it's rumored to have cost $30 million to produce.) If anyone in Hollywood or the *Times* for that matter was expecting all of the word of mouth to be a magic bullet for marketing and set records for its opening weekend, expectations were set too high.

The willingness of everyday people to get involved and participate will not replace traditional marketing, nor will it solve all existing marketing problems. It is a supplement, a booster. It may spell the difference between profit and loss, recognition and obscurity.

Since *Snakes on a Plane* was a first in many ways, it became a convenient target for skeptics threatened by its unconventional openness. Traditional Hollywood filmmakers learned that giving fans a stake in the outcome of films elevates word of mouth among creative and well-connected fans who will drive box-office results. *Snakes* was arguably more successful than it probably would have been otherwise; we saw the film during its opening weekend and it was pretty campy but in a fun way, like *Rocky Horror* but without the singing. What struck us most, though, was that the audience had a great time, especially when they said, in unison, Sam Jackson's infamous line about the motherfucking snakes on the motherfucking plane, then all laughed together. It was a real moment, and everyone knew it.

In 2006, a teenager calling herself "Lonelygirl15" posted a self-made video to YouTube. Talking directly to the camera, she said she was homeschooled, her parents were strict and very religious, and that her friend "Daniel" helped her with the video. Each of her subsequent videos told a story, often about her and Daniel, who had a crush on the beautiful and smart "Bree," as she called herself. But Bree wasn't romantically interested in Daniel, and that became the basis for many of her quirky videos. Very quickly, because of her movie-star good looks and ability to tell stories and talk about teen-atypical subjects like the physicist Richard Feynman, Lonelygirl15 became one of YouTube's amateur stars. Each of her video posts was viewed hundreds of thousands of times. Many posts had more than 1,000 comments, which is a remarkable number for anyone who is in the business of blogging.

Almost from the beginning, though, skeptics posted comments to each video, positing that some things did not add up. All of her videos were wonderfully lit. She was homeschooled but her very strict parents were oblivious to her videoblogging. "Daniel" seemed to spend a lot of time in Bree's bedroom with the door closed. Someone had trademarked "Lonelygirl15." People who sent Bree e-mails reported they didn't always come from the same e-mail address. She only talked in generalities about her religion, which took on the dark tones of a cult. Plus, it all seemed *too* professional. Bree was too good to be true.

It turns out the skeptics were right. The charade collapsed in September 2006 when the *Los Angeles Times,* then later the *New York Times,* breathlessly reported that Lonelygirl15 was really Jessica Rose, a young actor who'd graduated from drama school and was part of a fiction dreamed up by screenwriters. The talent firm Creative Artists Agency conspired with the filmmakers, who went to great lengths to cover their tracks. Authenticity is hard to fake, as any actor will tell you, and the natural intuitiveness of the human condition has a nose to sniff out a fake when we haven't willingly surrendered our disbelief. If the reader comments on the *New York Times'* website about its unmasking of Lonelygirl15 are any indication, the backlash to the deception was strong.

Throughout this book, we have described the various results borne from the power of one. Social media make it possible for one person to launch a domino effect of word of mouth that quickly sets off triggers of interest or alarm. The most successful work in this new world of media comes from a place of authenticity, not calculated deception or stealth marketing. In our estimation, those who set out to create "viral videos" face greater risks of failure because their intention is contrived at conception. Artifice is what social media combats. Nestled among the masses are plenty of amateur detectives, ready to strip away the varnish of what isn't real or authentic. Social media is the antidote to campaign-based thinking.

Those who think and plan in terms of campaigns are often unconcerned with what matters most toward true, unadulterated growth: loyalty. Loyalty is the real goal in the age of amateur culture and citizen marketers. The citizen marketers are demonstrating their loyalty by devoting their time and resources toward their hobby work. The independent bloggers and podcasters who have built impressive audiences are filled with their own loyal followers. Lonelygirl15 had loyal fans and created buzz, certainly, but now she is but a comic-book version of a person. Her creators are the successors to the minds behind the *Blair Witch Project,* which employed similar sleight of hand only to fade back to into obscurity. Bree had plenty of fans, but now they must contend with the deception and reset their expectations of what she represents, for it's certainly not reality. As a medium, YouTube made everyone real. Now YouTubers must contend with the inevitable copycats bound to follow in the path of Bree's fictional account of being a girl. If he were alive, McLuhan would probably laugh at all of the histrionics.

The hobbyist work of the citizen marketers is based on keeping it real. They demonstrate a conscious or unconscious belief in social altruism, driven by a belief system that the more a citizen marketer contributes to the greater good, the more valuable their contribution becomes. They are part of the mesh of the greater swath of fabric that interlocks everything together. The fabric of a safety net has an open texture, and no part of the fabric is more important than the other. The design of mesh ensures the fabric is evenly spaced. With this in mind, it is the open and transparent nature of shared production that enhances and illuminates what companies strive for but often misunderstand: loyalty.

Loyalty is a medium to growth. Among companies, loyalty can be a loosely used word and concept. Often its context is a "get the 10th sandwich free" card or frequent-purchaser rewards system. Those are common efforts, but they are more accurately called incentive programs. The casino chain Harrah's operates a very successful effort incentive program. Using swipe cards, the company tracks how customers spend money in casinos and offers incentives along the way to encourage them to keep their money in the company's properties. Each day, the company gathers a tremendous amount of data that teaches the company what its customers are doing and how it should respond. Their "walletshare" expansion is working; customers spent 43 percent of their annual gambling budgets at Harrah's properties in 2002, up from 36 percent when the program began. The company calls the program "Total Rewards." Not Total Loyalty. Harrah's smartly pairs their rewards program with a strong focus on customer service. One does not replace or supersede the other. Incentives and rewards are not always within the grasp of companies and organizations. The reward is the experience itself.

So how do we put loyalty into context in the age of the citizen marketer? Merriam-Webster defines *loyal* as "faithful to a private person to whom fidelity is due. Faithful to a cause, ideal, custom, institution, or product." For organizations hoping to inspire loyalty, a dependency or action is missing from that definition. Author and consultant Fred Reichheld proposes a standard for businesses: "The willingness to make an investment or personal sacrifice to strengthen a relationship." That definition helps measure the willingness of customers, advocates, and evangelists to do something, to become engaged with an organization. Counting the number of people who involve themselves with your organization—not just belong to it or buy from it—is a powerful measure of action beyond the sale. Beyond the membership. Beyond the donation.

Social media makes relationships easier to create and maintain because of participation, and participation is the fabric. People are bound together, but there's plenty of room to breathe. Participation is the future of marketing. Indeed, Peter Kim of research firm Forrester advocates that participation be added to the well-established four P's of marketing (product, price, place, and promotion). That's a fitting idea and worth pursuing inside the classrooms of business schools around the world, for social media makes it easier and less expensive for George Masters, Jeff Jarvis, Bowiechick, and all of the other 48 million American content creators to become publishers, spread messages, and build communities. It's already happening. The forces of democratization ushered in by the Internet make it so. The forces of democratization have made some online tools free, or almost free, because many are built and maintained by volunteers. Mashup the number of people online with the principles of democracy, especially freedom of expression and what is produced, are new business models, some of which are based on a participatory, vote-driven culture. Votes equate demand, and citizens determine the future. Their governance is real, not just hype. Their involvement is their loyalty. Like a meme with all of its built-in instructions, it turns out that loyalty is contagious.

Rags Vadali and Sonja Youngwith, two bright stars at the University of Chicago's Graduate School of Business, were our research assistants for *Citizen Marketers*. Their intelligence, enthusiasm, and ability to unearth data and academic research while providing necessary context for our project was invaluable, especially considering they were students with demanding loads of classes, homework, and school projects.

We thank Professor Puneet Manchanda of the University of Chicago's Graduate School of Business for his guidance during this project, too.

We graciously thank Professor Matthew McConnell (retired) for his insightful comments and guidance with the manuscript. His keen observations helped refine and improve every chapter.

For this book, we solicited a group of readers from our blog to become the book's peer-review committee. They read turbulent early drafts and generously provided comments, ideas, and suggestions that improved the book and its structure by, we estimate, a magnitude of three. We recognize and thank Tom Bonner, Maryann Devine, Phil Gerbyshak, Christina Kerley, Peter Kim, Matt Lindenburg, Przemek Piotrowski, Chuq Von Rospach, Todd Sattersten, Tracy Stevens, Chris Thilk, David Thomson, and Lance Weatherby. Special thanks to Peter Kim for coming up with the term "Firecrackers" that describes one of the four types of citizen marketers. We had originally termed the group "One-Hit Wonders" but Peter's "Firecrackers" idea was perfect.

We thank Sean Moffitt, who writes the BuzzCanuck blog, for pointing us toward the motorcycle outlaw group the 1 Percenters. A big thank you to all of the readers of our blog, Church of the Customer. Some of the work found in this book first appeared on our blog; it's almost impossible not to be influenced by the comments of people who respond directly or indirectly supporting an idea or criticizing it. For those who synthesize our work via our blog, a big, big thank you.

We thank all of the citizen marketers who generously gave us their time and attention in person, on the phone or via e-mail: Asif Alibhai, David Bott, Chris Cardinal, Matt Feidler, Brian Finkelstein, Armand Frasco, Eric Karkovack, Michael Marx, George Masters, McChronicles, Thomas Middleditch, Dave Muscato, Red Cart Romance, Jim Romenesko, and Fernando Sosa.

We thank the leaders of companies who graciously answered our many questions: Jakob DeHart, Jake Nickell, and Jeffrey Kalmikoff of Threadless; Steve Dembo, Scott Kinney, Coni Rechner, Steve Sidel, and Betsy Whalen of Discovery Education; Dick Costolo and Traci Hailpern of Feedburner; Scott Wilder of Intuit; Gina Clark and Patrick Seybold of Logitech; Kevin Rose of Digg; Steve Safran of *LostRemote.com;* Caterina Fake and Bradley Horowitz of Yahoo; Mena Trott of Six Apart; Erik Kalvianen of ProductWiki; Jeff Sandquist of Microsoft; Asa Dotzler of Mozilla; Melisa Tezanos of General Motors; and RJ Stangherlin of the Discovery Educator Network.

We thank authors and researchers who graciously shared their time and work with us: Steven M. Gelber, author of *Hobbies;* Max Kalehoff and Jonathan Carson of Nielsen BuzzMetrics; and Charlene Li and Peter Kim of Forrester Research.

This is our second book with Kaplan. We are big fans of Maureen McMahon, Kaplan's dynamic publisher. Her unflagging support and close involvement with the book has meant everything to us. Our editor, Karen Murphy, kept us on track and focused throughout the project. Her optimism is contagious. Special thanks to other members of the Kaplan team, including (but not limited to) Julie Marshall, Courtney Goethals, and Samantha Raue. Angela Hayes and Mark Fortier of Goldberg McDuffie were the wizards of publicity. Special thanks to Shelley Dolley for her assistance with tasks too numerous to mention. A special nod to John Moore and Paul Williams, who spent time with us in 2004 as we first fleshed out the concept of *Citizen Marketers.*

Finally, a heaping sack o' thanks to Todd Sattersten for his ongoing feedback, support, and friendship. His mission is to change the world of publishing. We have no doubt he will.

Introduction

Page vii
The song that George Masters used for his "ad" was "Tiny Machine" by the Darling Buds.

The basis of us saying that the color palette and imagery in George Masters's "ad" could have fit in with Apple's branding is based on the company's original rainbow-hued logo. Of course, Masters was taking liberties with Apple's imagery because he wasn't working on behalf of the company. And his work didn't jibe with Apple's now-ubiquitous iPod campaign that features the silhouette of an iPod wearer, the product's white ear bud cords hanging down against a colorful background. Incidentally, that branding campaign inspired at least one business: *iPodMyPhoto.com,* which offered to take any photo and convert it into an iPod-looking "ad." Apple is such a powerful force on culture that even its advertising work inspires an aftermarket of businesses.

Page viii
Wired's Leander Kahney studiously and religiously follows Apple. His article, "One Home-Brew iPod Ad Opens Eyes," in *Wired News,* December 13, 2004, helped signify the arrival of user-created content.

Masters and his iPod ad were featured on CNBC, *Wired* magazine, and the *New York Times.*

500,000 views of the iPod ad is a conservative estimate. George Masters said his website recorded more than 250,000 downloads, and *Wired.com* editor Leander

Kahney reported a similar number of views. Since Masters made his video downloadable, the total number of views does not account for how many people posted it to their own websites, including several other news-related websites.

Page xi
Jeff Jarvis has collected all of his posts about his Dell experience on his Buzz-machine.com blog. *buzzmachine.com/archives/cat_dell.html.*

Page xii
Business Week followed Dell's problems throughout 2005 and 2006. The first article it wrote was "Dell: Facing Up to Past Mistakes," by Louise Lee, *Business-Week,* June 19, 2006.

By using the stock market calculator tool at Yahoo (*finance.yahoo.com*), one finds that Dell stock closed at 41.25 on July 21, 2005. Dell stock on July 12, 2006, closed at 22.38.

Page xiii
The customer service makeover Dell undertook was profiled nicely, again, by *Business Week:* "From Servers to Service: Dell's Makeover," by Louise Lee, *Business Week,* May 19, 2006.

The quote about hoping "to learn and improve by listening to customers" comes from the Dell blog, something the company primarily employed at first as a product promotional tool. Bloggers promptly vilified it by not addressing the customer service issues that had been welling up for the past year. The writers of the Dell blog handled the criticism well (by not getting angry back) and started to address the issues. The Dell blog eventually changed its URL to *Direct2Dell.com* because the previous URL, *one2one.com,* was often mistyped and led viewers to a porn site.

The blogger B.L. Ochman described Dell's telephone call to her: *www.whats nextblog.com/archives/2006/07/dell_called_me_well_knock_me_over_with_a _feather.asp.*

Chapter 1: Filters, Fanatics, Facilitators, and Firecrackers

Page 1

A. N. Whitehead's quote is from Erich Jantsch's book *The Self-Organizing Universe* (Oxford, England: Pergamon Press, 1980), p. 73.

Page 2

Quotes from Fiona Apple have been extracted from an *Entertainment Weekly* cover story that examined the drama behind the scenes of the Apple-Epic dispute: "The 'Extraordinary' Truth: After six years of silence, Fiona Apple finally reveals the real reason her mystery-shrouded 'Extraordinary Machine' took so long," by Karen Valby, *Entertainment Weekly,* September 23, 2005.

Page 3

It was probably coverage in the *New York Times* that finally convinced Epic to pay for the rerecording sessions: "Re-emerging after a Strange Silence," by Lola Ogunnaike, *New York Times,* September 2005.

The story of *FreeFiona.com* and the work of Dave Muscato are based on material on the FreeFiona Web site as well as interviews the authors conducted with Muscato via e-mail.

Page 5

The quotes from Dave Muscato are from interviews we conducted with him.

Quotes and some data about HackingNetflix blogger Mike Kaltschnee are courtesy of blogger Christina Kerley: "Yo Marketers: Hack This! (Blogger Q&A with HackingNetflix.com)," by Christina Kerley, CK's Blog, June 23, 2006. *www.ck-blog.com/cks_blog/2006/06/yo_marketers_ha_1.html.*

Page 6

Quotes and facts about Kaltschnee's work as a blogger writing about Netflix are from his blog, *HackingNetflix.com. hackingnetflix.com/netflix/2005/03/hacking_netflix.html.*

Page 8

All quotes from Jim Romenesko are from an e-mail interview we conducted with him in July 2006.

Page 9

All commentary quotes about Starbucks are from the StarbucksGossip blog. *starbucksgossip.com.*

John Moore's book is *Tribal Knowledge: Business Wisdom Brewed from the Grounds of Starbucks Corporate Culture,* published by Kaplan (2006). His quote is from his blog, Brand Autopsy. *brandautopsy.typepad.com/brandautopsy/2006/ 08/gossip_gossip_g.html.*

Page 10

Technology trade magazines have been kind to the Filters because they are often such reliable sources of information, customer usage, and story ideas. Harry McCracken's article can be found at *blogs.pcworld.com/treolog/archives/ 000657.html.*

We interviewed Asif Alibhai of *WatchMacTV.com* via email in July 2006.

Page 11

The quotes of the McChronicles blogger about the McDonald's store in the Haight-Ashbury district are from the McChronicles blog. *mcchronicles. blogspot.com/2006/07/haight-ashbury-mcdonalds.html.*

The quotes from the McChronicles blogger about why he does what he does and why he chooses to remain anonymous are from a series of e-mail interviews we conducted with him in November 2005. He said he was inspired to start his blog because of a blogging workshop hosted by the American Marketing Association at which coauthor McConnell was one of the speakers. McConnell remembers seeing the McChronicles blogger in the audience based on a picture he put on his Web site. So although the McChronicles blogger is mostly anonymous, he's not totally anonymous.

Page 12

Michael Marx, the Barq's blogger, talks about why he blogs about his favorite root beer in "I'm With the Brand," by Amy Corr, *MediaPost,* March 2006.

Page 13

John Frost talks about his being a "third generation Disney Fan" in his bio on his blog, *thedisneyblog.typepad.com/about.html.*

Frost says he started the Disney Blog because back in 2004, when he first heard about blogs, there were no Disney-related blogs in existence. *thedisneyblog .typepad.com/tdb/2006/06/welcome_typepad.html.*

Page 14

To see the video made by the Walt Disney World interns, go to *www.youtube.com/ watch?v=0NpHKsf8VKs&search=disney.*

The story about the lengths that *Angel* fans went to in trying the save the show came from "*Angel* fans try like the devil to revive show," by Bill Keveney, *USA TODAY,* April 12, 2004.

The fun facts about the crazy *Arrested Development* fans who sent stuff to Fox executives came from "The awful Bluths," by Mike Miliard, *Boston Phoenix,* February 18–24, 2005.

Three anonymous donors from the commercial spaceflight industry accounted for most of the $3 million. The story is documented here: "Star Trek campaign raises $3m," *BBC News,* March 2, 2005.

TV critic Mark Dawidziak wrote a column lamenting how HBO could cancel one of the best shows in TV history: "Al would have choicer words for what HBO's doin' here," by Mark Dawidziak, *Cleveland Plain Dealer,* June 11, 2006.

Page 15

HboNoMo.com is the site where, in two weeks, 654 HBO subscribers threatened to cancel their subscriptions if the pay cable channel did not bring back *Deadwood* for a fourth season. Our quote is from petition signer 404, Suzanne Siegel.

Chip Collins's *SaveDeadwood.net* story is detailed in *"Deadwood Dead?"* by Rebecca Dana, *Rolling Stone,* June 2, 2006.

See the *Variety* ad from *Deadwood* fans here: *savedeadwood.net/pledge.htm.*

HBO executives say they were inundated with angry e-mails from *Deadwood* fans: "*Deadwood* Gets a New Lease on Life," by Jesse McKinley, *New York Times,* June 11, 2006. We don't know, however, how many of them were filled with cussing.

Page 16

Full Contact Poker is an online poker community. One of the "off-topic forums" on the site discusses television shows: *www.fullcontactpoker.com/poker-forum/index.php?showtopic=62968.*

Page 17

W. Earl Brown's comments can be found at *boards.hbo.com/thread.jspa?threadID=300001145&messageID=700086589#700086589.*

Chip Collins, the *SaveDeadwood.net* founder, says that *Deadwood* fans weren't going down with out a fight in *"Deadwood* appears to be dead in the water for fourth season," by David Kronke, *LA Daily News,* May 28, 2006.

Page 18

The information and data about the Mini2 community is from the site *www.mini2.com.*

Page 20

We interviewed Matt Feidler by e-mail about his "Milk and Cereal" video in June 2006.

"Milk and Cereal" video received a brief but favorable mention in the *New York Times:* "Snap, Crackle, Sing," by Lisa Napoli, *New York Times,* August 26, 2004.

Page 21

A writer for Wikipedia calls the "Milk and Cereal" video an "internet meme," a buzzword phrase to describe the buzzword phrase "viral video." You can find the entry at *en.wikipedia.org/wiki/Milk_and_Cereal.*

Big brands were paying big money to sponsor NBC's *The Apprentice,* including Kraft Foods. Read more here: "The Donald excels at marketing Trump card," by Jonathan Bing, *Variety,* March 20, 2006.

The details of Post Grape-Nuts Trail Mix Crunch sponsorship of the *Apprentice* episode is from "Post, TV Guide and the Donald," by Neal Leavitt, *iMedia Connection,* June 7, 2006.

Page 22

Sales data about Post Grape-Nuts Trail Mix Crunch was supplied to us by Information Resources, Inc. The data is based on actual unique product codes scanned at checkout counters in supermarkets, drugstores, and mass merchandise outlets, excluding Wal-Mart.)

Page 23

E-mail from Logitech spokesman Patrick Seybold to the authors outlines sales increases due to the Bowiechick video.

Page 24

The *Nightline* piece was a thorough and solid examination of the Vincent Ferrari story, putting it into a context of things to come: "How the Web Flips 'Caveat Emptor': If the Marketplace Is a Shark Tank, Guess Who's Getting Eaten?" ABC News/*Nightline,* July 14, 2006. *abcnews.go.com/Nightline/story?id=2194970&page=1.*

Page 25

The behind-the-scenes story of the Oscar Mayer jingle is extracted from a wonderful piece Doug Ode wrote for Madison, Wisconsin's daily newspaper: "Hot Dog! Oscar Ode Still Lives," by Doug Ode, *Capital Times,* Jan. 14, 2005.

Page 26

BIGresearch conducts regular surveys with its survey group, which consists of people of various ages. More information about its influential study about word of mouth as the most influential media can be found at *www.marketwire.com/mw/release_html_b1?release_id=104538.*

A 2005 Yankelovich "Study on Marketing Receptivity" finds that most people are just really sick of advertising. *www.crm2day.com/news/crm/114029.php.*

Page 27

See the Lincoln Fry Blog (*http://lincolnfry.typepad.com*). Even though there were exactly three total posts to the blog (two on February 5, 2005, and one on February 6), the blogger, "Mike," writes: "Thanks, everyone, for all the support. Liz and I are amazed at the traffic this blog has gotten. But I'm getting overwhelmed by the volume of comments coming in. I'm afraid I just don't have the time to police this blog all day and night. As it is, my e-mail inbox is constantly filling up. So I had to close this blog to any additional comments."

Page 28

The story of Kaltschnee's outreach to Netflix is detailed on the HackingNetflix blog, *www.hackingnetflix.com/netflix/2004/06/bloggers_corpor.html.*

For more commentary on the Hacking Netflix blog, see *BusinessBlogConsulting.com, www.businessblogconsulting.com/2004/06/hackingnetflixc.html*

For even more commentary on the Hacking Netflix blog, see *Micropersuasion.com, steverubel.typepad.com/micropersuasion/2004/06/blogger_gives_n.html.*

Page 29

Kaltschnee's quote can be found at *www.hackingnetflix.com/netflix/2004/06/bloggers_corpor.html.*

Page 30

See "E-mail Response Times Lag Still," by Coreen Bailor, Destination CRM, Sept. 1, 2005. *www.destinationcrm.com/articles/default.asp?ArticleID=5361.* A study by BenchmarkPortal, a company that analyzes call centers, found that small- and medium-sized businesses (SMBs) delivered poorer online service than larger businesses. Among North American SMBs with revenues of $10 million and $250 million, 51 percent failed to respond to e-mails at all, and 70 percent did not respond within 24 hours, compared to 41 percent of enterprises not responding at all and 61 percent not responding within 24 hours. When they do respond, things get worse: 79 percent of SMBs responded with an inaccurate and/or incomplete answer, compared to 83 percent of enterprises. See the second study from the "State of eService Benchmarking Series" released by BenchmarkPortal in June 2005.

The book *The Cluetrain Manifesto,* by Christopher Locke, Rick Levine, and Doc Searls, covers a good deal of this. The book's well-known catchphrase, "Markets are conversations," has become a guiding principle for those organizations dependent upon word of mouth. Read the entire "manifesto" online at *www.cluetrain.com.*

Chapter 2: The 1 Percenters

Page 31
The opening quote is from *Hell's Angels,* by Hunter S. Thompson, Ballantine Books, 1996, p.13.

Page 33
The story of the fateful day in Hollister, Calif., that gave rise to the legend of the 1 Percenters and their badge of "social status" is from a wonderful and authoritative article: "A Brief History of 'Outlaw' Motorcycle Clubs," by William L. Dulaney, *International Journal of Motorcycle Studies,* November 2005.

Bryan Noonan examines the culture of an "outlaw" motorcycle club in Kansas City with his article "Live Free & Die: After Kansas City's first generation of outlaw bikers rides off into the sunset, who will replace them?" *Pitch,* June 30, 2005.

The 2005 Wikipedia visitor stats come from comScore Media Metrix, an online measurement company, in a press release entitled "Star-Struck Observers Drawn to Space Shuttle Launch Online, Reports comScore Media Metrix," August 26, 2005.

Page 34
The number of Wikipedia content creators is documented in *The Wealth of Networks* by Joachi Benkler, Yale University Press, 2006.

The numbers of people who have created an article in the first five years of Wikipedia's existence came from founder Jimmy Wales, in a speech in October 2005: *www.hyperorg.com/blogger/mtarchive/wikipedias_long_tail.html.*

The 2006 Wikipedia visitor stats come from comScore Media Metrix in a press release entitled, "Spring Fever Drives Web Traffic as Americans Explore Travel, Educational Testing and Classifieds Sites," April 17, 2006.

The fact that Wikipedians had created 864,000 articles is from "Growing Wikipedia Revises Its 'Anyone Can Edit' Policy," by Katie Hafner, *New York Times,* June 17, 2006.

The number of articles in *Encyclopaedia Britannica* came from its Web site: *store.britannica.com/shopping/product/detailmain.jsp?itemID=665&itemType= PRODUCT&iProductID=665.*

Page 35

The visitor numbers for Yahoo Groups come from Nielsen//NetRatings, May 2006.

Bradley Horowitz discusses his observations of "Creators, Synthesizers, and Consumers" of Yahoo Groups on his blog: *www.elatable.com/blog/?p=5.*

The QuickBooks Community data is from email and in person interviews with Scott Wilder, Group Manager, QuickBooks Software and Small Business Services, at Intuit, June-August, 2006.

E-mail discussion with David Bott, administrator of *TiVoCommunity.com,* in July 2006. Bott says that the average number of unique visitors to the site is 1.1 million, and the average number of new discussion threads per month is 4,000. He was not able to determine how many people create the 4,000 threads. But if we can assume that the most people who could create 4,000 threads is 4,000, then 4,000 divided by 1.1 million is .36 percent. This says that less than 1 percent of visitors are creating the 4,000 threads. The low percentage may be caused by a "Chit Chat" area on the site (where site members chat about anything other than TiVo), which easily has the most threads on any of the forum's sections, and those threads are started by a very small number of people.

Page 36

The data about ProductWiki is courtesy of Erik Kalviainen of ProductWiki. He also found that the number of actions per contributing visitor is about 1.4. That means a contributor wrote an entry or edited one, wrote a comment, or contributed a tap. The other interesting data point about ProductWiki is its strong growth: in April 2006, the site hosted 36,242 visitors; in July 2006, it hosted 75,901 visitors. The contribution rates and percentages for all four months, though, largely remained the same.

Based on data provided to us by Jeff Sandquist, one of Channel 9's founders and a technical evangelist for Microsoft's Platform Strategy Group.

The data about the Discovery Educator Network was provided to us by Discovery Education. Steve Dembo's quotes are from interviews we conducted with him in person, on the phone, and via email June–August of 2006.

Page 37

The Juran Institute Web site has a concise history of Joseph Juran and his many contributions to the world of business management and theory. *www.juran.com /lower_2.cfm?article_id=21.*

Page 38

The examples of power law distributions come from the academic paper "Power Laws, Pareto Distributions and Zipf's Law," by M. E. J. Newman, *Contemporary Physics,* Taylor & Francis, September 2005.

Clay Shirky's work has been highly influential in guiding a lot of thinking around social media. His essay described "the long tail" of power laws and was the inspiration for the development of that idea, which Chris Anderson later turned into a book by the same name. The essay we quoted can be found here: *www.shirky.com/writings/powerlaw_weblog.html.*

Page 39

Descriptions of Wikipedia contributors came from "Many Contributors, Common Cause: Wikipedia Volunteers Share Conviction of Doing Good for Society," by David Mehegan, *Boston Globe,* February 13, 2006.

Wikipedia contributor Branford Stafford's comments are from "The Idealists, the Optimists, and the World They Share," by David Mehegan, *Boston Globe,* February 13, 2006.

Page 40

Read Seigenthaler's scathing review of Wikipedia here: "A False Wikipedia 'Biography,'" by John Seigenthaler, *USA TODAY,* November 29, 2005.

Nicholas Garr writes about the "death" of Wikipedia on his blog: *www.roughtype .com/archives/2006/05/the_death_of_wi.php.*

"Wikipedia's accuracy judged to be as good as that of *Britannica,*" by Dan Goodin, the Associated Press, Dec. 15, 2005. *seattletimes.nwsource.com/html/nationworld/ 2002684602_wikipedia15.html.*

Page 41

Data about Internet usage in the U.S. is from "Broadband Adoption 2006," Pew Internet & American Life Project, March 2006. The survey results are based on the compiled results of two separate surveys. The first was based on a random sample of 3,011 adults, 18 and older, and had a sampling error of 1.9 percentage points. The second was based on a random sample of 4,001 adults, 18 and older, and had a sampling error of 1.7 percentage points. Pew is a nonpartisan think tank that produces 15–20 reports per year. Its support comes from the Pew Charitable Trusts, which were established by the children of Sun Oil founder Joseph N. Pew and his wife, Mary Anderson Pew. Pew's reports and descriptions of its methodologies are freely available from its Web site: *pewinternet.org.*

Page 43

One blogger details what happens when a post from his blog appeared on the front page of Digg: "The Digg Effect," *hrmpf.com/wordpress/44/the-digg-effect.*

Read about Digg's status (and the other 24 most popular Web sites) in "Valley Boys: Digg.com's Kevin Rose leads a new brat pack of young entrepreneurs," by Sarah Lacy and Jessi Hempel, *BusinessWeek,* August 14, 2006.

The numbers behind Digg's growth are from "Digg 3.0 to Launch Monday: Exclusive Screenshots and Stats," by Michael Arrington, proprietor of the technology news blog *TechCrunch.com.* Arrington said his figures are from an interview with Digg founders Jay Adelson and Kevin Rose.

The figure that AOL paid for Weblogs, Inc. was reported in "AOL to buy Weblogs Inc., courts bloggers," by Kenneth Li and Eric Auchard, *Reuters,* Oct. 6, 2005.

Page 44

Quotes from Netscape's Jason Calacanis about his offer to pay top social bookmarkers are from his blog: *www.calacanis.com/2006/07/18/everyones-gotta-eat-or-1-000-a-month-for-doing-what-youre.*

Calacanis later posts on his blog the details about his effort to hire the top social bookmarkers: *www.calacanis.com/2006/08/02/the-first-10-navigators-weve-hired-three-of-the-top-12-digg-us/.*

The Adam Smith quote is from his seminal and oft-quoted work *The Wealth of Nations,* written in 1776 (Modern Library Edition,1994), p. 15.

The Samuel Johnson quote is from James Boswell's *The Life of Samuel Johnson,* Everyman's Library, 1993, p. 641.

Page 45

Lessig is founder and chair of the Creative Commons and a board member of the Electronic Frontier Foundation. He writes extensively about "non-commercial culture" in his book *Free Culture: How Big Media Uses Technology and the Law to Lock Down Culture and Control Creativity* (Penguin, 2004).

The poverty threshold for a two-person household was $12,490 in 2004, according to the U.S. Department of Health and Human Services *(aspe.hhs.gov/ poverty/04poverty.shtml)*.

Wages for fast-food workers can be found at *Salary.com: swz.salary.com/salary-wizard/layoutscripts/swzl_compresult.asp?NarrowCode=HS02&Narrow-Desc=Restaurant+and+Food+Services&JobTitle=Counter+Attendant&JobCode=HS08000003&geo=U.S.%20National%20Averages.*

Page 46
The idea of the "read-write culture" and the quotes from Lessig come from *News.com*'s coverage of the Wikimedia 2006 conference: "Lessig seeks legal ground for content exchange," by Martin LaMonica, *News.com,* Aug. 4, 2006 *(news.com.com/Lessig+seeks+legal+ground+for+content+exchange/2100-1038_3-6102451.html?tag=nefd.top)*.

Page 47
The idea of the "unimportance of the distribution of income" is from *The Economic Approach to Human Behavior,* Gary S. Becker, University of Chicago Press, 1978.

Michael Marx talks about why he writes the Barqsman blog in "I'm With the Brand," by Amy Corr, *MediaPost,* March 2006.

Kevin Rose, one of the founders of Digg, discussed the democratizating forces of the site in an e-mail with the authors in August 2006.

Page 48
Tyson Hy talks about why he didn't accept Jason Calacanis's offer to be a Netscape paid bookmarker on his blog *(tysonhy.com/2006/07/another-persons-thoughts-on-this-so.html)*.

Try applying the rule of the 1 Percenters to the total number of company employees and measure it against how many people contribute to the knowledge-management system. Or tally the total number of members of a church or non-profit organization and discover how many of them volunteer to lead committees or perform operational duties.

Page 49

The plight of the land cultivators in Greece is discussed in *Constitution of Athens,* by Aristotle, London, 1891.

Solon is quoted as to why he resisted calls to become dictator of Greece in *The Life of Greece,* by Will Durant, Simon and Schuster, 1939, p. 117.

"*Efcharisto*" meant "thank-you" in ancient Greek.

Page 50

The quote about the meaning of "politeia" is from *A Company of Citizens* by Brook Manville and Josiah Ober, Harvard Business School Press, 2003, p. 10.

Chapter 3: The Democratization of Everything

Page 51

The "Shakespeare Navigators" at ClickNotes are fun: *www.clicknotes.com/hamlet/Three4.html.*

The quotes from Kara Swisher about Pathfinder, as well as Time Warner confidently calling it "the world's best Web site" are from Swisher's book: *There Must Be a Pony in Here Somewhere: The AOL Time Warner Debacle and the Quest for the Digital Future,* by Kara Swisher, Three Rivers Press, 2004, p. 82.

Page 52

The quotes from the Time Warner spokersperson are from "Time Warner to shutter Pathfinder," by Jim Hu, *News.com* (part of CNET Networks), April 26, 1999. *news.com.com/2100-1023-224939.html.*

The number of Yahoo visitors is from "MySpace overtakes Yahoo Mail," *CNNMoney.com,* July 12, 2006.

Page 53

Cubs' president Andy MacPhail is quoted from "Wrigley faces checkup as more concrete falls," by Gary Washburn, *Chicago Tribune,* July 23, 2004.

The Cubs' 2006 ticket prices is mentioned in "Cubs a Winner for Tribune," by Michael A. Hiltzik, *Los Angeles Times,* June 21, 2006.

Page 54

The Quotations Page Web site has the Sun Tzu quote: *www.quotationspage. com/quote/24269.html.*

Page 55

More from Mena Trott can be found at the *Fast Company* magazine blog: *blog.fastcompany.com/archives/2004/07/23/business_transparency.html.*

In the *The 9/11 Commission Report,* the quote about information not being shared is on page 353. The quote about implementing a network-based information-sharing system is on page 400. The full report is available in book form or online as a PDF: *www.9-11commission.gov/report/911Report.pdf.*

Page 56

The fact about 70 countries having laws that ensure the right to request and review public documents is from "We Need Fewer Secrets," by Jimmy Carter, *Washington Post,* July 3, 2006.

Page 57

Tim Berners-Lee posted a summary of his "WorldWideWeb project" to an online newsgroup on August 6, 1991. You can view his "executive summary" of the project at: *groups.google.com/group/alt.hypertext/msg/395f282a67a1916c.*

Page 58

The Institute for Interactive Journalism at the University of Maryland awarded Adrian Holovaty its Batten Award: *www.j-lab.org/batten05winnersrelease.shtml.*

Page 59

Watch the "Brokeback to the Future" mashup on YouTube: *www.youtube.com/ watch?v=8uwuLxrv8jY.*

Watch the neat mashup of "Shining" on YouTube: *www.youtube.com/watch? v=Z11B9L2awVA.*

Page 60

The quote from Doug Adams on the issue of trusting what is on the Internet is from "How to Stop Worrying and Learn to Love the Internet," by Douglas Adams, *Sunday Times,* August 29, 1999.

The two Kuhn quotes are from *The Structure of Scientific Revolutions,* by Thomas S. Kuhn, University of Chicago Press, 1962 (third edition).

Page 61

The Kuzweil quotes are from *The Singularity Is Near: When Humans Transcend Biology,* by Ray Kurzweil, Viking, 2005, p. 50.

Page 62

All of the statistics we cite by Pew Internet about the number of broadband users and content creators come from its comprehensive report, "Home Broadband Adoption 2006," May 26, 2006 *(pewinternet.org)*.

Page 63

Figures about DSL adoption rates in countries from around the world are from DSL Forum report, March 2006.

"Broadband and Unbundling Regulations in OECD Countries," by Scott Wallsten, American Enterprise Institute/Brookings Institute Joint Center for Regulatory Studies, June 2006. Round out the top 10 were (6) Finland, (7) Norway, (8) Canada, (9) Sweden, and (10) Belgium. The United States trailed Japan (11).

Page 64

All of the price data about digital cameras and their accessories is from Mintel, "Digital Cameras: March 2006 Report."

Page 65

"The coming Web video shakeout: The number of YouTube-like services now stands at a staggering 173—and in April alone 3 outfits got $30 million in funding. Who will survive?" by Om Malik, *Business 2.0,* June 20, 2006.

Webcam industry market share statistics are courtesy of TechWeb: *www.techweb.com/wire/hardware/174403304*.

Logitech webcam sales cited are based on a fiscal year that ends March 31. More information: *ir.logitech.com/secfiling.cfm?filingID=1193125-06-116374*.

Page 66

The statistics about kids using electronic and computer equipment is from "NPD Study: More and More Children Using Consumer Electronics," by Beth Snyder Bulik, *Advertising Age,* May 31, 2006.

Adoption rates of POTS and the cell phone are from *The Singularity Is Near: When Humans Transcend Biology,* by Ray Kurzweil, Viking, 2005, pg. 50.

Cell phone industry growth figures are from Mintel, Consumer Communications: July 2005 Report.

Data on 3G network subscribers is from Mintel, 3GToday, July 2005 report.

Page 67
The statistics about how many people use their cell phones to vote in television contests is from "How Americans use their cell phones," Pew/Internet & American Life Project, April 3, 2006.

The number of American kids and Europeans who own mobile phones is from Forrester Research: "Social Computing," by Chris Charron, Jaap Favier, and Charlene Li, February 13, 2006.

Page 68
More information about Nicholas Negroponte's work to create what's called the sub-$100 computer (although it's not quite below $100) can be found on *News.com*. We cited facts from "$100 laptop gets working prototype," by Jonathan Skillings, *News.com,* May 24, 2006. *news.com.com/100+laptop+gets+ working+prototype/2100-1005_3-6076351.html?tag=nl.*

Page 69
The data about kids and technology is, again, from Forrester's "Social Computing" report.

Chapter 4: Everyone Is a Publisher;
Everyone Is a Broadcaster

Page 71
Marshall McLuhan's theories are a guiding force for understanding the role of media as an influence on culture. See *Understanding Media: The Extensions of Man,* by Marshall McLuhan, Mentor/New American Library, 1964.

For more on whether the *Acta Diurna* were written under the authority of the Roman government, see *penelope.uchicago.edu/Thayer/E/Roman/Texts/secondary/ SMIGRA*/Acta.html.*

For even more on the *Acta Diurna,* see *The Press and America,* by Michael Emery and Edwin Emery, Prentice Hall, 1988. Around the same time, similar bulletins appeared in parts of China. But Chinese news was reserved for government officials only, not all citizens.

Page 72

For more on Gutenberg, see *Gutenberg: How One Man Remade the World with Words,* by John Man, Wiley, 2002.

Page 73

The quote from Elizabeth L. Eisenstein about Martin Luther's Protestant Reformation is from *The Printing Press as an Agent of Change* by Elizabeth L. Eisenstein, Cambridge University Press, 1979, pg. 303.

Page 75

Our quotes about McLuhan come from his essential book *The Medium Is the Massage,* by Marshall McLuhan and Quentin Fiore, Touchstone, 1967. "The television is a voting booth," pg. 22; "Our official culture is striving to force the new media to do the work of the old," pg. 94.

More on Justin Hall's isolation can be found in the *San Francisco Chronicle: www.sfgate.com/cgi-bin/article.cgi?file=/c/a/2005/02/20/MNGBKBEJO01.DTL.*

See the full interview with Hall on the Neomarxisme blog: *www.pliink.com/mt/marxy/archives/000517.html.*

Page 76

LiveJournal shares a good deal of data about itself on its website at *livejournal. com/stats.bml.*

Mena Trott talks about the history of her blogging tool, Movable Type, on her company's blog: *www.sixapart.com/about/history.*

We talked about the blog tool market in an interview with Forrester analyst Charlene Li on July 14, 2006.

Page 77

The latest figures about the number of blogs in the world can often be found on the personal blog of Technorati CEO David Sifry: *www.sifry.com/alerts/.*

Pew Internet & American Life Project's "Who's Online" study shows the current demographics of Internet users. The data we looked at for this chapter was from their February–April 2006 survey.

Nielsen Buzzmetrics 2005–2006 Consumer-Generated Media Engagement Monitor study discusses that "influentials" (a term coined by RoperASW as meaning that 10 percent of the population that influences other people) appear at a greater rate in the online population than the general population.

Page 78

LiveJournal had a practice of sharing a good deal of its data publicly before Six Apart purchased it in 2006.

For more on Windows Live Spaces, see a Microsoft press release: *www.microsoft.com/presspass/press/2006/may06/05-24SpacesLargestPR.mspx.*

The data and hypotheses that Hurst formed are found in "24 Hours in the Blogosphere," by Matthew Hurst, American Association for Artificial Intelligence, 2006, *www.aaai.org.*

Page 79

News of the MySpace acquisition is discussed here in "News Corp in $580m internet buy," *BBC News,* July 19, 2005, *news.bbc.co.uk/2/hi/business/4695495.stm.*

News of the Weblogs Inc. acquisition is discussed in "AOL to buy Weblogs Inc., courts bloggers," by Kenneth Li and Eric Auchard, *Reuters,* October 6, 2005.

Page 80

Quotes from Technorati's Dave Sifry and data about Technorati are from *Sifry.com* and "State of the Blogosphere, August 2006." *www.sifry.com.*

Dave Sifry's quote about the human limits of blogging are from Sifry.com: *www.sifry.com/alerts/archives/000436.html.*

"Internet Usage Statistics—The Big Picture," Miniwatts Marketing Group, 2006. The figures come from data aggregated by World-Gazetteer, Nielsen/NetRatings, the International Telecommunications Union, and local NICs. *www.internetworldstats.com/stats.htm.*

"A Manifesto for Networked Objects—Cohabiting with Pigeons, Aphids and Aibos in the Internet of Things," by Julian Bleecker. *research.techkwondo.com/files/WhyThingsMatter.pdf.*

New Scientist, "Pigeons to Set Up a Smog Blog." February 2, 2006: *www.new scientisttech.com/article/mg18925376.000.html.*

Page 81.

See the pigeon photos and more at: *www.pigeonblog.mapyourcity.net.*

Page 82

You can find the "Real Deadwood Podcast" on iTunes or at: *www.realdead woodpodcast.com.*

The "Meandering Mouse" Disney-fan podcast can be found on iTunes and at: *meanderingmouse.com.*

The facts and quote about NPR's podcast program and its future plan were supplied by Eric Nuzum, NPR's director of programming and acquisitions, during a telephone interview with the authors in May 2006.

Page 83

The Nielsen Analytics percentages are from its press release for its report "The Economics of Podcasting."

Radio listenership numbers are from "Digital Listening Growing, Radio Slipping," *CNET,* May 13, 2005.

Page 84

Paul Farhi profiles Rocketboom in the June/July 2006 issue of the *American Journal Review.*

Subscribe to Microsoft's press relases on its Web site: *www.microsoft.com/ presspass/rss/PressReleases.xml.*

Page 87

The percentage of email that was spam was discussed in "In the Fight against Spam E-mail, Goliath Wins Again," by Brian Krebs, *Washington Post,* May 17, 2006.

The story of ITV being cancelled is from "Time Warner to Shutter ITV effort," by Jeff Peline, January 15, 1995: *news.com.com/2102-1017_3-279393.html?tag =st.util.print.*

Page 88

The first DVR is chronicled in "A Bit of TiVo History," by Jim Barton, *ACM Queue: www.acmqueue.org/modules.php?name=Content&pa=show page&pid=53 &page=4.*

TiVo has said that 96 percent of its subscribers say they will never give up their TiVo services, as cited in "Talking' About a TiVolution," by Ryan Underwood, *Fast Company,* June 2002: *www.cnn.com/2006/TECH/internet/07/12/myspace. reut/index.html.*

Page 91

The number of bands on MySpace is mentioned in this interview: "Q&A: MySpace Founders Chris DeWolfe and Tom Anderson," by Natalie Pace, *Forbes,* January 4, 2006. There are probably more new bands on MySpace every week than can be accurately counted.

For more on Friendster, see "His Space," by Spencer Reiss, *Wired,* July 2006.

MySpace became the most-visited U.S Web site in July 2006, overtaking Yahoo Mail, as described by "Report: MySpace top single U.S. Web site," by *Reuters,* July 12, 2006. Yahoo disputed this contention by traffic-monitoring service Hitwise. "The Yahoo network is made up of many domains and it is not accurate to compare *MySpace.com* to just Yahoo's e-mail site," a company statement said. Like songs on the *Billboard* 100, number-one Web sites will come and go.

The Google-MySpace deal is outlined in "Google signs $900m News Corp deal," *BBC News,* August 7, 2006: *news.bbc.co.uk/1/hi/business/5254642.stm.*

Page 92

The info on YouTube reaching more people than other sites is from Alexa Internet, a subsidiary of *Amazon.com.* Alexa Internet operates *Alexa.com,* which makes Internet traffic from data sent by users of the Alexa Toolbar freely available from its Web site. Alexa anonymously collects the Web-site usage of its "millions" of users (the company does not provide an exact figure) and aggregates that data into a sample set. Alexa does have its critics; it works only with Windows computers and only with Microsoft's Internet Explorer browser and may skew toward technically savvy users rather than the average Internet user. It's probably best to view Alexa data not as a scientific sample but as a measure of trajectory. Alexa seems to work well when comparing the relative reach of two similar Web sites.

YouTube stats are detailed in "YouTube serves up 100 million videos a day online," *Reuters,* July 16, 2006.

Hitwise ranked YouTube as the 39th most popular Web site in July 2006. By the time you are reading this, the ranking could be very different. The Hitwise ranking is mentioned in "Hollywood casts eager eye on YouTube," by Thomas K. Arnold, *USA TODAY,* July 5, 2006.

Page 95
Read more about Cyworld in "E-Society: My World Is Cyworld," by Moon Ihl-wan, *Businessweek,* September 26, 2005.

Chapter 5: Hobbies and Altruism

Page 97
Learn more about Carlisle's status as a major trucking hub at *www.cen-tralpa.org/archives/02may3miracle.html.*

Page 98
Learn more about the Cars of Carlisle events at *www.carsatcarlisle.com/aboutus/index.asp.*

The number of cases of Coke Classic sold in 1997 is from *Beverage Digest,* February 12, 1998.

Page 99
The publisher of *Beverage Digest* talks about why Surge didn't sell in "Fan Club Seeks to Revive Surge Soda," *Associated Press,* April 18, 2005.

All quotes from Karkovack are from discussions we had with him in person or via e-mail in May–August 2006.

Page 101
The description of the SaveSurge Hall of Fame is listed on the Web site. See *www.savesurge.org/surge/halloffame/hofs.html.*

Page 102
The mission for *Vaultkicks.org* is mentioned on its Web site: *www.vaultkicks.org/about_site.php.*

Page 103

The marketing tactics used by Coca-Cola to launch Vault are available on the Coca-Cola website: *www2.coca-cola.com/presscenter/nr_20060217_americas_vault.html.*

The number of hours that teens spend on the Internet versus television is from the 2003 Yahoo "Born to Be Wired" study: *http://docs.yahoo.com/docs/pr/release1107.html.*

Page 106

The quotes from Steven M. Gelber in *Hobbies: Leisure and the Culture of Work in America* (Columbia University Press, 1999) are on pgs 2–4. He also spoke with us by phone from his home in Santa Clara, California.

Winter's Web site is *www.starbuckseverywhere.net.*

Winter's quotes about collecting Starbucks are from "Flights of Fancy," by Michelle Griffin, *Age,* January 5, 2006.

Page 107

Winter's quote about Starbucks coffee being consistent is from "Better latte than never to achieve goal," by Matt Viser, *Boston Globe,* November 28, 2005.

Winter's quote about too much coffee is from "Seeing the World on Ten Coffees a Day," by Daniel Roth, *Fortune,* July 12, 2004. The quote from the Starbucks spokesperson is also from this article.

Page 108

McDonald's response to the McChronicles bloggers is described in "Spreading the Word: Corporate evangelists recruit customers who love to create buzz about a product," by James Pethokoukis, *U.S.News & World Report,* December 5, 2005.

The reference to McLuhan saying that "tools shape us" is from his quote "We become what we behold. We shape our tools and then our tools shape us." The quote is from *Understanding Media: The Extensions of Man,* by Marshall McLuhan, Mentor/New American Library, 1964.

Page 109

The phrase "everyday market helping behavior" was coined in the essay "Everyday Market Helping Behavior," by Linda L. Price, Lawrence F. Feick, and

Audrey Guskey, *Journal of Public Policy and Marketing,* fall 1995. Their essay refers to the history of research conducted about people relying on friends, casual acquaintances, and even total strangers for recommendations. Our categories of altruism, personal relevance, common good, and evangelism are an adaptation of categories they identified for market-helping actors.

Page 110

Quotes from Tocqueville are from *Democracy in America,* by Alexis de Tocqueville. The "forming associations" quote is on pg. 513. The "towns are like great meeting houses" is on pg. 279.

Page 111

Read more about the study involving freeloaders and sanctioning in "The Competitive Advantage of Sanctioning Institutions," by Ozgur Gurerk, Bernd Irlenbusch, and Bettina Rockenbach, *Science,* April 7, 2006.

Page 112

All quotes from Armand Frasco are the result of interviews we conducted with him in the summer of 2006.

Page 115

The George Will quote is from "TV for Voyeurs" by George F. Will, *Washington Post,* June 21, 2001.

Read about the birth of *America's Funniest Home Videos* on the Museum of Broadcast Communications' Web site: *www.museum.tv/archives/etv/A/htmlA/ americasfun/americasfun.htm.*

Page 116

See the homemade McNuggets' ad at: *www.youtube.com/watch?v=XSZ6k3QIsAk.*

Page 117

We interviewed Middleditch and Sosa in June 2006.

Page 120

The quotes about Millennials come from *Millennials and the Pop Culture: Strategies for a New Generation of Consumers,* by William Strauss and Neil Howe, LifeCourse Associates, 2006.

Chapter 6: The Power of One

Page 121

The chapter's opening quote is from *The Hero with a Thousand Faces,* by Joseph Campbell, Princeton University Press, 1968, p. 243.

Casey Neistat talks about a small backlash of e-mails from Apple fans after he posted the "iPod's Dirty Secret" video in "Battery and Assault," by Hank Stuever, *Washington Post,* December 20, 2003.

Page 122

Casey Neistat talks about feeling exploited by Apple in "Brothers Make Apple See iPod Light," *CBS Evening News,* January 3, 2004.

Casey Neistat and his brother Van talked about the origin of their video on *Your World with Neil Cavuto,* Fox News, January 9, 2004.

See the Neistat video and the brothers' commentary about it at: *http://neistat. com/pages/projects.htm.*

Casey talks about Apple calling him on *CBS Evening News,* January 3, 2004.

Page 123

Apple's response is quoted from "Battery and Assault," *Washington Post.*

Read about memes in Richard Dawkin's book *The Selfish Gene,* Oxford University Press, 1976, p. 192.

Page 124

The meme replication process, consisting of assimilation, retention, expression, and transmission, is described in the paper, "What Makes a Meme Successful? Selection Criteria for Cultural Evolution," by Francis Heylighen, in the *Proceedings of the 15th International Congress on Cybernetics,* 1998.

Page 126

Finkelstein talks about the response from Comcast to his video in "Your Call Is Important to Us. Please Stay Awake," by Ken Belson, *New York Times,* June 26, 2006.

Nielsen BuzzMetrics' "2005–2006 Consumer Generated (CGM) Engagement Monitor" report profiles online content creators and their habits and attitudes.

Page 128

The Forbes award for the Slave to Target blog is here: *http://www.forbes.com/bow/ b2c/review.jhtml?id=7741.*

Page 129

Wikipedia has a good history of the term *astroturfer:* see *http://en.wikipedia.org/ wiki/Astroturfer.*

The Target fan blogger talks about stuff at the stores $1 Shop here on the blog: *http://slavetotarget.blogspot.com/2006_06_04_slavetotarget_archive.html.*

She writes about the Coffee Smarts trivia game here: *http://slavetotarget. blogspot.com/2006_04_30_slavetotarget_archive.html.*

Page 130

She writes about Isaac Mizrahi's ill-fitting designs here: *http://slavetotarget. blogspot.com/2006/04/isaac-youre-killin-me.html.*

She writes about Target "selling out" with their new high-end designer line here: *http://slavetotarget.blogspot.com/2006/05/sellin-out.html.*

Her "selling out" quote from the blog is featured in "Where Target Is Always 'Tar-zhay,'" by Ylan Q. Mui, *Washington Post,* June 21, 2006.

She talked about her blog's traffic numbers, how she knows she is driving sales, and why she thinks the company won't talk to her in a phone interview with the authors on June 29, 2006.

Page 131

Target's response to our inquiry about the Slave to Target blog was from Carolyn Brookter, director of corporate communications for Target Corporation, via e-mail on July 20, 2006.

Page 132

The Bellagio-style Diet Coke and Mentos geyser video is mentioned in "Diet Coke 'experiment' gives Mentos a surge in publicity," by Suzanne Vranica and Chad Terhune, *Wall Street Journal,* June 12, 2006.

See the very Vegas-like Grobe-Voltz Diet Coke and Mentos video here: *www.revver.com/video/27335.*

Steve Spangler's book *Fizz Factor: 50 Amazing Experiments with Soda Pop* was published in 2003 but is out of print. There's a chance you could buy a used copy on Amazon or directly from Spangler at *www.stevespanglerscience.com/product/1419*.

Page 133
The reactions to the Diet Coke and Mentos videos by their respective companies are from "Mixing Diet Coke and Mentos Makes a Gusher of Publicity," by Suzanne Vranica and Chad Terhune, *The Wall Street Journal*, June 12, 2006.

Page 134
The description of Flickr's algorithm is from Stewart Butterfield's entry, "The New Things," on the Flickr blog, August 1, 2005: *blog.flickr.com/flickrblog/2005/08/the_new_new_thi.html*.

We talked with Bradley Horowitz in his office at the Yahoo Research lab in Berkeley, California, on June 23, 2006.

Flickr's "interestingness" system led us to Trey Ratcliff. Among the millions of photos on Flickr, his are often featured as the most interesting. We loved his work, so we asked him to shoot a photo of us for this book's cover jacket. He's not a full-time professional photographer, though. He spends most of his time as the CEO of a gaming company in Austin, Texas.

Chapter 7: How to Democratize Your Business

Page 135
William Gibson's quote is from an interview he gave to NPR's *Talk of the Nation* program, November 30, 1999. *discover.npr.org/features/feature.jhtml?wfId=1067220*.

The failure rate of new products is mentioned by a Forrester analyst in "Consumers Driving New Product Innovation," by John P. Mello Jr., *EcommerceTimes.com*, June 6, 2006.

Page 136
The 2006 revenue was expected to total $20 million, as reported to us by the Threadless founders during an interview in June 2006.

Page 139

Visit the Loves Threadless fan blog at *www.lovesthreadless.com.*

All quotes and comments from Jake Nickell are from our conversation with him in June 2006.

Susumu Ogawa and Frank T. Piller explore the realm of possibilities the Threadless model could have on other industries in their article, "Reducing the Risks of New Product Development" in the winter 2006 *MITSloan Management Review.*

Page 140

You can find the 21 one-page primers on the fundamentals of democracy produced by the U.S. Government here: *usinfo.state.gov/products/pubs/principles.*

Page 144

You can watch the amateur films inspired by Converse's Chuck Taylor sneakers at *www.conversegallery.com.*

The quote from Converse marketing chief Erick Soderstrom and the report of Converse sales being up 12 percent in the second quarter of 2005 was reported in "Advertising Of, By, and For the People," by David Kiley, *BusinessWeek,* July 25, 2005. The description of Steve Daniels' Converse film was also noted here.

David Maddocks, Converse's vice president of global marketing, calls the Converse Gallery campaign a "tremendous success" in this article: "Marketers' New Idea: Get the Consumer to Design the Ads," by Suzanne Vranica, *Wall Street Journal,* December 14, 2005. The Ban deodorant campaign and results are also documented in this article.

"Consumer-created Video Ads Boost Converse Sales," by Marc Graser, *AdAge,* February 7, 2005. Also from the article: "Compared to August 2003 figures, traffic to *www.converse.com* surged 66 percent soon after Converse Gallery was launched last August, with more than 1 million people visiting the site and 400,000 people visiting *ConverseGallery.com* directly. December traffic increased nearly 200 percent from the year-ago month. And viewers have turned into customers. Sales have doubled Converse's online shoe sales doubled in just a month after Converse Gallery was introduced, with much of those purchases occurring after people viewed the spots. The company was able to track just how many people clicked on a link at the end of a short that took them to the Converse store on the site."

Page 145

Alex Sandell talks about the counterculture nature of the Chuck Taylor All-Stars in "The Day Nike Took over the World: Counter-Culture for Sale!" for the *Juicy Cerebellum* online zine, 2003: *www.juicycerebellum.com/converse.htm.*

The history of the Chuck Taylor All-Stars is from the Converse Web site: *www.insidehoops.com/converse-history.shtml.*

The Web traffic results from the Ban deodorant campaign are from "Thinking Outside the (Mail)box," by Alexandra DeFelice, *CRM Magazine,* March 2006.

Page 146

The Ban deodorant campaign results are from "Marketers' New Idea: Get the Consumer to Design the Ads," by Suzanne Vranica, *Wall Street Journal,* December 14, 2005.

The Ban contest Web site is at *banit.feelbanfresh.com.*

Page 147

Blake Ross, one of the cofounders of Firefox, talks about the number of "Spread Firefox" registered members on the Naked Conversations blog: *redcouch.typepad .com/weblog/2005/03/interview_with_1.html.*

Asa Dotzler of Mozilla discussed the Firefox user-generated video contests with us via e-mail in August 2006.

Page 148

Winners of the Kansas City radio station listener-created commercial contest are interviewed about their video in "20 grand was in the bags," by James A. Fussell, *Kansas City Star,* May 7, 2006.

Page 149

The description of the video or page is from the Wal-Mart "School Your Way" Web site: *schoolyourway.walmart.com.*

Page 150

The Wal-Mart "School Your Way" contest was reviewed by a reporter and teenagers in "Wal-Mart Tries to Be MySpace. Seriously," by Mya Frazier, *Advertising Age,* July 17, 2006.

This theory and idea was developed in full by C. K. Prahalad and Venkat Ramaswamy in their book *The Future of Competition: Co-Creating Unique Value with Customers,* Harvard Business School Press, 2004.

Cammie Dunaway, chief marketing officer of Yahoo, talked about the "Hips Don't Lie" video contest during her keynote presentation at the Brandworks University conference on May 25, 2006.

Page 151
Jay Frank, the head of programming and music relations for Yahoo Music, talks about how many times the fan-version of the "Hips Don't Lie" video was viewed in "For Shakira, First Came the Album, Then Came the Single," by Maria Aspan, *New York Times,* June 12, 2006.

Page 152
Read a review of the Sundance debut of the Beastie's concert film here: *www.cinematical.com/2006/01/21/sundance-review-awesome-i-fuckin-shot-that.*

BBC movie critic Matt McNally said the fan concert film "is 89 minutes of shared, spontaneous, and noisy joy" in his July 4, 2006 review: *www.bbc.co.uk/films/2006/06/26/awesome_i_shot_that_2006_review.shtml.*

Beastie Boys' Adam Yauch (aka MCA, aka Nathanial Hornblower), the director of the band's fan concert film *Awesome: I Fuckin' Shot That,* talks about film in "Awesome, I Sat Through That," by Jason Silverman, *Wired News,* January 23, 2006.

Piaggio Group discusses their reasons for starting the Vespaway blog at *www.vespausa.com/VespaBlogs/blogFAQ.cfm.*

The VespaWay blog is found at *www.vespaway.com.*

Page 153
Paolo Timoni, chief executive of Piaggio USA, talks about the Vespaway blog in "Corporate Marketers Try Out Blogs," by Brian Steinberg, *Wall Street Journal,* May 3, 2005.

The Lego Mindstorms co-creation story is detailed in "Geeks in Toyland," by Brendan I. Koerner, *Wired,* February 2006.

Page 155

VCR penetration figures are gleaned from "Video Is Here to Stay," by Everett Rogers, *Media & Values,* winter 1998. *www.medialit.org/reading_room/article 260.html.*

Internet penetration in schools is described in "Internet in Nearly Every School," by Kathie Felix, *Multimedia Schools,* January 1, 2001.

Page 156

Coni Rechner's quotes about the DEN are based on multiple interviews we had with her throughout 2006.

Page 157

Susan Little's comment about the Discovery Educator Network was in the comments section for a post on the DEN blog: *discoveryeducation.typepad.com/ discovery_educator_networ/2006/06/going_to_necc_j.html#comments.*

Page 158

All of Steve Sidel's comments are the result of an interview we conducted with him in June 2006.

Scott Wilder talked with us about the QuickBooks Community in June 2006.

The number of QuickBooks customers is mentioned here: *www.network world.com/newsletters/sbt/2006/0619networker3.html.*

Page 160

Microsoft CEO Steve Balmer is well known in the technology industry for his "developers, developers, developers" riff at an internal company event. The footage was remixed with a techno soundtrack and became a viral video. See the original footage at *www.youtube.com/watch?v=kaJREvJW72g.* See the remixed video at *video.google.com/videoplay?docid=- 4677979070070993985&q=balmer.*

Microsoft's Jeff Sandquist told us about Channel 9 content creation in e-mail interviews in July and August 2006.

Jeff Sandquist talks about communities as music festivals on his blog: *www.jeff sandquist.com/CommunitiesAreMusicFestivals.aspx.*

Page 161

Gary Hamel's and C. K. Prahalad's "The Core Competence of the Corporation" (*Harvard Business Review,* Vol. 68, no. 3, May–June 1990, p. 79) is a must-read.

Page 162

David Ellis's reaction to the SoaP title is mentioned in "An Unfinished Flick's Online Fang Club," by Jacqueline Trescott, *Washington Post,* April 8, 2006.

Roger Ebert trashes *Snakes on a Plane* while interviewed for *The Current,* with host Anna Maria Tremonti and reporter Aaron Brindle, CBC Radio-Canada, May 4, 2006.

Samuel L. Jackson talks about the changing SoaP title and rating in "Listening to the Hissing," by Josh Tyrangiel, *Time,* May 1, 2006. David Ellis talks about tailoring the movie for the fans.

The best SoaP fan song is "SoaPSong," by Subatomic Warp and DC Lugi (aka David Coyne): *www.snakesonablog.com/swp/wp-content/uploads/2006/02/DCLugi_SoaPSong.mp3.*

Page 163

Screenwriter-blogger Josh Friedman said he used *Snakes on a Plane* as his "Zen koan." A Zen koan is a paradox to be meditated upon that is used to train Buddhist monks to abandon ultimate dependence on reason and force them into gaining sudden intuitive enlightenment. See *hucksblog.blogspot.com/2005/08/snakes-on-motherfucking-plane.html.*

Page 164

This is Brian Finkelstein's first post to Snakes on a Blog: *www.snakeson ablog.com/2006/01/12/snakes-on-a-blog.*

We interviewed Finkelstein in his Washington, D.C., apartment on June 12, 2006.

Finkelstein reported the statistics on the following blog: *www.snakeson ablog.com/2006/07/14/snakes-on-a-blog-ix.*

Page 166

Finkelstein talks about New Line's hands-off approach to fan citizen marketers in "*Snakes on a Plane* blog buzz forces Hollywood into overdue attitude adjustment," by Neva Chonin, *San Francisco Chronicle,* June 12, 2006.

This was one of the first major media outlets to write about the SoaP citizen marketers: "*Snakes on a Plane* a Web Phenomenon," by Erin Carson, *Associated Press,* April 20, 2006.

Page 167

Chuck Klosterman thinks producers tailoring SoaP to fan's wishes is a terrible idea and says so in "The *Snakes on a Plane* Problem," by Chuck Klosterman, *Esquire,* August 2006.

Page 168

John Heffernan thinks it's a great idea to collaborate with movie fans. He says why in "Call it YouHollyWood," by Ryan Pearson, *ASAP AP,* June 26, 2006. So, take that, Chuck.

See "*Snakes:* A Letdown After the Hype," by Sharon Waxman, Aug. 21, 2006, *The New York Times.*

Box Office data is from Nielsen EDI, Inc. via the *New York Times,* Sept. 12, 2006 (*www.nytimes.com/pages/movies/boxoffice/weekend_us/index.html*).

Conclusion

Page 172

"Well, It Turns Out that Lonelygirl Really Wasn't," by Virginia Heffernan and Tom Zeller Jr.," *New York Times,* Sept. 13, 2006.

The *Times'* blog has more on Lonelygirl15, plus reader comments: *screens. blogs.nytimes.com/?p=77.*

Page 174

Harrah's frequent-purchaser system is described in "Make Every Customer More Profitable: Harrah's Entertainment, Inc.," by Margaret L. Young and Marcia Stepanek, *CIO Insight,* Dec. 1, 2003.

The definition of loyalty that we prefer is one described in the article "The One Number You Need to Grow," by Frederick F. Reichheld, Harvard Business Review, December 2003. His article was expanded to a full-length book, *The Ultimate Question,* (Harvard Business School Press, 2006).

We are indebted to a roster of researchers and big thinkers whom we have relied on to make sense of social media in the context of media history. Their books served as reference guides and guidance counselors in our work with *Citizen Marketers*.

Becker, Gary S. and Kevin M. Murphy. *Social Economics: Market Behavior in a Social Environment*. Boston: The Belknap Press of Harvard Business School Press, 2000.

Becker, Gary S. *The Economic Approach to Human Behavior*. Chicago: University of Chicago Press, 1976.

Benkler, Joachia. *The Wealth of Networks*. New Haven: Yale University Press, 2006.

Bryson, Bill. *A Short History of Nearly Everything*. New York: Broadway Books, 2003.

Dawkins, Richard. *The Selfish Gene*. Oxford, England: Oxford University Press, 1976.

De Geus, Arie. *The Living Company: Habits for Survival in a Turbulent Business Environment*. Boston: Harvard Business School Press, 2002.

Durant, Will. *The Story of Civilization: Part II, The Life of Greece*. New York: Simon and Schuster, 1939.

Eisenstein, Elizabeth L. *The Printing Press as an Agent of Change, Vols. 1 and 2.* Cambridge, England: Cambridge University Press, 1979.

Emery, Michael and Edwin Emery. *The Press and America, Sixth Edition.* Upper Saddle River, NJ: Prentice Hall, 1988.

Gelber, Steven M. *Hobbies.* New York: Columbia University Press, 1999.

Johnson, Steven. *Everything Bad Is Good for You: How Today's Popular Culture Is Actually Making Us Smarter.* New York: Riverhead Books, 2005.

Kuhn, Thomas S. *The Structure of Scientific Revolutions, Third Edition.* Chicago: University of Chicago Press, 1996.

Kurzweil, Ray. *The Singularity Is Near: When Humans Transcend Biology.* New York: Viking, 2005.

Lessig, Lawrence. *Free Culture: How Big Media Uses Technology and the Law to Lock Down Culture and Control Creativity.* New York: The Penguin Press, 2004.

Man, John. *Gutenberg: How One Man Remade the World with Words.* Hoboken: John Wiley & Sons, 2002.

McLuhan, Marshall and Quentin Fiore. *The Medium Is the Massage.* New York: Touchstone, 1967.

McLuhan, Marshall. *The Gutenberg Galaxy: The Making of Typographic Man.* Toronto: University of Toronto Press, 1962.

McLuhan, Marshall. *Understanding Media: The Extensions of Man.* New York: Mentor/New American Library, 1964.

Moulitsas, Markos and Jerome Armstrong. *Crashing the Gate.* White River Junction, VT: Chelsea Green, 2006.

Ober, Josiah and Brook Manville. *A Company of Citizens.* Boston: Harvard Business School Press, 2003.

Pfeffer, Jeffrey and Robert I. Sutton. *Hard Facts, Dangerous Half-Truths & Total Nonsense: Profiting from Evidence-Based Management.* Boston: Harvard Business School Press, 2006.

Prahalad, C. K. and Venkat Ramaswamy. *The Future of Competition: Co-Creating Unique Value with Customers.* Boston: Harvard Business School Press, 2004.

Rogers, Everett M. *Diffusion of Innovations, Fifth Edition.* New York: Free Press, 2003.

Smith, Adam. *The Wealth of Nations.* New York: Modern Library, 1994.

Strauss, William and Neil Howe. *Millennials and the Pop Culture: Strategies for a New Generation of Consumers.* Great Falls, VA: Life Course Associates, 2006.

Von Hippel, Eric. *Democratizing Innovation.* Cambridge, MA: The MIT Press, 2005.

Zakaria, Fareed. *The Future of Freedom.* New York: Norton, 2003.

Share the message!

Bulk discounts
Discounts start at only 10 copies and range from 30% to 55% off retail price based on quantity.

Custom publishing
Private label a cover with your organization's name and logo. Or, tailor information to your needs with a custom pamphlet that highlights specific chapters.

Ancillaries
Workshop outlines, videos, and other products are available on select titles.

Dynamic speakers
Engaging authors are available to share their expertise and insight at your event.

Call Kaplan Publishing Corporate Sales at 1-800-621-9621, ext. 4444, or e-mail kaplanpubsales@kaplan.com

PUBLISHING